CONTENTS

ACKNOWLEDGEMENTS

It has been a wonderful journey compiling this anthology, and many people have helped to create this groundbreaking two-spirit theatre anthology. First and foremost, I want to express my gratitude to Muriel Miguel, Kent Monkman, and Waawaate Fobister for being the inspiration for this anthology. It is their daring artwork that gave birth to this book. I want to thank Annie Gibson, Playwrights Canada Press publisher, for believing in this project the moment it was suggested. I am appreciative of Annie's flexibility and willingness to support a collective approach to the anthology. Thanks to Playwrights Canada Press staff members Blake Sproule and Mandy Bayrami, who were integral to the completion of the anthology. I would like to also thank my partner, Jessica Eden, for all her positive support and helpful suggestions throughout this process.

Thanks to Deborah Ratelle, Muriel's partner and business manager, who acted as intermediary for email exchanges and was instrumental in editing the *Hot 'n' Soft* script. I also want to convey how much I enjoyed and appreciated editing *Hot 'n' Soft* with Muriel over our many phone conversations. A special thank you to Ann Haugo for introducing me to Deborah and Muriel. Thanks to Brad Tinmouth, Kent's manager, for sending along all the materials needed for the anthology. I want to give a big thanks to Richard Hill, Sharon Day, and Falen Johnson for their willingness to write introductions to each of the pieces, and to Tomson Highway for writing a fantastic opening piece and for his often humorous emails. Finally, thanks to Adrian Stimson for his fabulous cover artwork.

I would like to thank my mentors and colleagues Marlis Schweitzer, Theresa May, and Christina Accomando for their constant support of my work. Thanks also to my community for the unwavering encouragement: Nicole Z., Rodney, Jaese, Lara, Nora, Gayle, Becky, Olive, Jon, Shana, Miriam, Carlisle, Kristin, Tisa, Saul, Helene, Melanie, Vishakha, James, Erica, Janet, Maria, Jennifer, Aleta, CJ, Shira, Willoughby, Nicole F., Marlon, Sue, Phil, Judy R., Judy S., Marlette, Marylyn, Dave L., Dave M., Lorena, Loren, Jessica, Debbe, Margaret, Kathy, Eva, Fyre, Glen, Ian, Lila, Karen, Kristina, Victor, Nikki, and Tonye. I am deeply grateful for all your love and support.

WHERE IS GOD'S WIFE? OR IS HE GAY?
BY TOMSON HIGHWAY

The difference as I see it goes like this . . .

Christianity, as who doesn't know it, arrived in North America in 1492. In Europe where, of course, it came from, it had predecessors. As a monotheistic system of thought, that is to say, it had polytheistic roots. It sprang from the Romans and THEIR predecessors, the Greeks. Meaning to say that—if within monotheism—there exists one god only, "mono" meaning "one" in ancient Greek, "theos" meaning "god," then the system that preceded it and from whence it sprang had many gods, and goddesses, "poly" meaning "many" in Greek. There was Zeus (the immediate predecessor of the present Christian "God the Father," known as Jupiter in the Roman system), Apollo, Dionisis (Bacchus), Poseidon (Neptune), Hermes (Mercury), etc. And then there were "the girls": Zeus's wife, the mother goddess, Hera—yes, this male god actually had a wife, known in the Roman system as Juno—Demeter (Ceres in Roman), Artemis (Diana), Aphrodite (Venus), etc. And each god and goddess had a role in taking care of the universe and all its inhabitants. There was a god (Apollo) who took care of the sun, there was a goddess (Hera) who took care of the Earth, there was a god (Poseidon) who took care of the sea, there was a goddess (Demeter) who took care of grain and the harvest. There was even a goddess who took care of sex, of sexual plea-sure between human beings; you come face to face with her when you have an orgasm, at that moment, that is to say, when you reach heaven on Earth. Her name was Aphrodite. There was even room in that system of thought for a cross-gender god. His/her name was Hermaphroditus. Offspring of the messenger god who escorted people to the land of the dead (Hermes) and his sister Aphrodite, the goddess of love, of sexual pleasure, he, legend has it, had the sexual organs of both male and female, double pleasure for the bitch, that is to say.

But then these systems were absorbed by Christianity to the detri-ment of all those gods. But one. And all those goddesses. Somehow in there, when the polytheism of the Greeks and the Romans was replaced by Christianity's monotheism, the idea of divinity in female form dis-appeared. Because within monotheism there exists one (mono) god (theos) only, and that god is male. And heterosexual, meaning to say that, within this superstructure, anyone who is not male heterosexual—i.e., women and gays—is out of luck, is in danger. Our question as Native writers and thinkers being: When this male god arrived here in 1492, why did he come alone? Where was his wife? Where was his girlfriend? Or is he gay? How can a male god create the universe completely on his own without help from a female? Does sexual pleasure actually exist in this system? Are we allowed to have orgasms? Or do we go to hell if we do?

The argument, of course, goes much further, but to cut to the chase, this male, heterosexual god arrived in North America in 1492, very recently when you consider the system of spirituality that it met, which goes back eons. And to find out how old that system, pantheism, is, you HAVE to speak at least one Native language with complete fluency, for that's where such secrets lie . . . within the warp and weave of linguistic structure. "Pan" meaning "all" in ancient Greek. In any case, pantheism comes to us from a time before mankind had anthropomorphized the idea of divinity, "anthro" meaning "man" in Greek, "morph" meaning "form." Meaning to say that it comes to us from a time in human history before gods had human shape in our imaginations. For instance, the Christian god the Father is an old man with a big white beard and a thunderbolt in hand hiding behind a puffy white cloud glaring down at us here on Earth, waiting for us to make one wrong step. All the Greek (and Roman) gods had human form, Poseidon with his trident, Aphrodite with her belt of gold, Hermes with the wings on his ankles being just three we know best. And Zeus with his big white beard and silver thunderbolt. Sound familiar?

In pantheism, contrariwise, the idea of divinity has NO human form. It is simply an energy, a "great spirit" that functions like an electrical bolt that shoots its way through the universe animating everyone and all that it touches and/or passes through, which is one reason why pantheistic languages don't even have a "he" or a "she." In that system, therefore, we are all he/shes. As is god, one would think. Meaning to say that, within the pantheistic system, there is at least room for the idea of divinity in female form. And in two-spirit form, just as with Hermaphroditus in the Greek system.

Monotheism, moreover, is obsessed with gender. Its languages— English, French, German, etc.—divide the universe into that which is male, that which is female, and that which is neuter, with the hierarchy of power going from the top to the middle to the bottom; a phallic design, that is to say. Languages that have a pantheistic base, on the other hand—that is the Aboriginal languages of North America—ignore the concept of gender completely. They divide the universe, contrariwise, into that which is animate and that which is inanimate, that is, into that which has a soul and that which has none. So that a woman, man, dog, tree, rock, and even an ant all have equal status because they all have souls. They all sit on the circle of the living. And it is a circle, not a straight line, vertical or otherwise, but a circle. Only when they die—for instance when the man becomes a corpse or the tree becomes a chair or the rock becomes cement that becomes a sidewalk—do they get "translated" onto a CONCENTRIC circle, the circle of the non-living, the inanimate. But they have gone nowhere, not up to heaven, not down to hell. They're all still here. Meaning to say that the superstructure of pantheism is a circle. It is, that is to say, not a phallic design but a yonic design, "yonic" coming from the word "womb." And so goes the argument . . . eternally. It would fill ten books easy.

On the vertical STRAIGHT LINE of monotheism, therefore, there is room for two genders only, male and female, with the former having complete power over the latter. On the CIRCLE of pantheism, on the other hand, there is room for many genders. In the traditional Native sense that goes back eons—and to put it in too-simplistic terms—the man hunted, the woman gave birth and nurtured. And the people who were physically, emotionally, psychologically, and spiritually equipped for neither role—that is, the people who were both male and female, who were spiritual hermaphrodites—they took care of the emotional and spiritual life of the family, the community. In the boring, and very violent, black-and-white world of the two-gender system, that is to say, they injected all the colours of the rainbow. Where would Cher be without them? Who would make her dress, do her hair, her makeup? That's our job. These "spiritual hermaphrodites," that is to say, were the artists, the priests, the visionaries. They had, that is to say, not only a sacred but an essential role in the community. Because, for instance, the male and female heterosexual were way too busy raising six, eight, ten children—in my family there were twelve, of which I am the eleventh—it fell into the hands of the "two-spirits" to take care of the elders. That is our job. Here in France, here where I live winters, the elderly get dumped into seniors' homes and are forgotten by their children who are, as I say, too busy leading their own lives. So while I write here in my office on the hill by the sea, my husband of almost thirty years spends his days down the hill and up and down the coast playing bridge with them. And teaching them how to play it. Best way to avoid Alzheimer's because, as I hope you know, bridge is all about memory, it is all about memorizing the movement of all fifty-two cards around that table. To look at it from the other extreme perspective, the fag-basher who kills my husband (and then goes home to beat his wife, with complete approbation from the monotheistic male system; nothing wrong with that, according to that system), that fag-basher, in killing my husband, makes those elders suffer. And because the elders suffer, we all suffer.

These plays, in any case, open the door to such enlightening, necessary debate. They are important plays; one step, and a very important one, in our fight as two-spirits to take back the dignity that was wrested from us by monotheism, by Christianity. And I hope it is only the first one of many. May god-as-female come back to us. May our Mother come back to us . . . *Igwaani kwayus* (Cree for "Damn rights, baby").

—Tomson Highway
France, Spring 2013

INTRODUCTION

The sacred fire doesn't burn only for straight folks. We queer folks dance around the fire, too, our voices strong, our hearts full, our spirits shining. We have gifts of healing to bring too.
—Daniel Heath Justice

It is springtime as I write this introduction. The hummingbirds have returned to find nectar in the foxgloves and fuchsias in my yard. It is a time of renewal, birth, and regeneration. At present, I am on Wiyot land—what is now called Arcata, California. European Americans and European Canadians came to Wiyot land in the mid-1800s in search of gold. As the gold-rush fever intensified, local militia routinely murdered Wiyot people, along with other local Native peoples. On February 26, 1860, during a seven-day World Renewal ceremony on Tuluwat Island, Wiyot people were massacred in three separate locations. Few survived and the murderers were acquitted. Today the Wiyot have reclaimed Tuluwat Island; they have since finished this World Renewal ceremony and are planning for future ceremonial dances. In addition, the Wiyot nation is actively working to teach younger generations their language, knowledge, and traditions.

Two-Spirit Acts: Queer Indigenous Performances is also an expression of renewal and of survival. The artists in this anthology are keeping two-spirit stories alive despite the demonization, subjugation, and elimination of two-spirit people and their histories by the colonial powers of Canada and the United States. Each of these artists celebrates Indigenous understandings of sexuality, gender, spirituality, and identity. Their collective art is a form of survivance,[1] a form of activism, a form of history-making that honours Indigenous people. Through storytelling, each artist offers an opportunity for healing and decolonization for both Native and non-Native communities.

This anthology celebrates the stories of two-spirit people, written by two-spirit artists. It represents three generations of two-spirit artists from multiple nations: Muriel Miguel is Kuna and Rappahannock, Kent Monkman is Cree, and Waawaate Fobister is Grassy Narrows. This book is a shared effort comprised of writings from Indigenous scholars, theatre artists, and activists including Tomson Highway, Sharon Day, Richard Hill, and Falen Johnson, along with the artwork of Adrian Stimson. *Two-Spirit Acts: Queer Indigenous Performances* is a collective that offers multiple perspectives of two-spirit art and brings a much-needed voice to conversations in theatre studies, Indigenous studies, and queer studies.

What does two-spirit mean? The word two-spirit was coined during the Native lesbian and gay movement of the 1990s to establish a space for coalitions and activism that integrated Native identities.[2] Unlike the words gay, lesbian, bisexual, trans, or queer, two-spirit is the only word that incorporates Indigenous cultural understandings. The two-spirit definition co-created by the editors of *Sovereign Erotics: A Collection of Two-Spirit Literature* is the most inclusive definition I have found:

---

1   Survival and resistance as defined by Gerald Vizenor.
2   More about this history can be found in Scott Morgensen's article "Unsettling Queer Politics: What Can Non-Natives Learn from Two-Spirit Organizing?," *Queer Indigenous Studies: Critical Interventions in Theory, Politics, and Literature*, ed. Qwo-Li Driskill, et al. (Vancouver: UBC Press, 2011), 132–38.

Two-spirit or two-spirited is an umbrella term in English that (1) refers to the gender constructions and roles that occur historically in many Native gender systems that are outside of the colonial binaries and (2) refers to contemporary Native people who are continuing and/or reclaiming these roles within their communities. It is also used . . . within grassroots two-spirit societies . . . [and is] meant to be inclusive of those who identify as two-spirit or with tribally specific terms, but also GLBTQ Native people more broadly.[3]

The artists in this anthology identify themselves as two-spirit, with Fobister specifically identifying as *agokwe*, an Anishnaabe term. Miguel additionally identifies as a lesbian and Fobister also identifies as gay.

Two-Spirit Acts: Queer Indigenous Performances opens with Muriel Miguel's *Hot 'n' Soft*, introduced by artist and activist Sharon Day. In *Hot 'n' Soft*, Miguel makes use of the Spiderwoman story-weaving structure, and moves seamlessly from recounting the events of her life to relaying coyote trickster tales and exploring lesbian erotica. Throughout the play, she not only claims her sexual desire, she does so without the shame of the "sexaphobic settler regime."[4] Miguel embodies an Indigenous understanding of sexuality—one that embraces sexuality as an important part of being alive. Next, Richard Hill introduces Kent Monkman's three pieces: *Taxonomy of the European Male*, *Séance*, and *Justice of the Piece*. Monkman exposes the eroticization, reification, and commodification of Indigenous people by the colonizers. He questions both the power and validity of the heteropatriarchy and exposes the fallacies of colonial history. Lastly, Falen Johnson introduces us to Waawaate Fobister's

---

3   Qwo-Li Driskill, et al. (Tuscon: U Arizona P, 2011), 4.
4   A term coined by Daniel Heath Justice in "Notes Toward a Theory of Anomaly," GLQ: *The Journal of Lesbian and Gay Studies* 16.1-2 (2010): 208.

play, *Agokwe*. Fobister's story examines Aboriginal and colonial beliefs systems with respect to two-spirit people. He also demonstrates the lasting effects of forced assimilation on Indigenous communities—which includes homophobia. In the end, Fobister reclaims an Anishnaabe understanding of two-spirit people and invites the audience to do the same.

Two-Spirit Acts: Queer Indigenous Performances honours storytelling as a living history. All three theatre artists share their knowledge of two-spirit people and their own lived experiences in their work. Together their stories expose the continued effects of colonization on Native communities while also honouring the resiliency of Native people. Miguel, Monkman, and Fobister ultimately support Indigenous sovereignty and world views. Their art is an invitation for us to collectively move away from the dominant paradigm in which logic is valued over intuition/imagination, competition over collaboration, male-centred over life-centred, and hierarchal over shared power. Miguel, Monkman, and Fobister challenge the greater community to "radically reimagine our futures"—one that is ultimately inclusive and life-affirming.[5]

---

5   Qwo-Li Driskill, "Doubleweaving Two-Spirit Critques: Building Alliances between Native and Queer Studies," GLQ: *The Journal of Lesbian and Gay Studies* 16.1-2 (2010): 70.

HOT 'N' SOFT

BY MURIEL MIGUEL

Muriel Miguel is Kuna/Rappahannock and is a founding member and artistic director of Spiderwoman Theater, the longest-running women's theatre company in North America. Muriel studied modern dance with Alwin Nikolais, Erick Hawkins, and Jean Erdman and was an original member of Joseph Chaikin's Open Theater.

She choreographed *Throw Away Kids* and *She Knew She Was She* for the Banff Centre and directed *The Scrubbing Project* with Turtle Gals Performance Ensemble and *Evening in Paris* with Raven Spirit Dance in Vancouver. As an actor, she performed in the off-Broadway hit, *The Lily's Revenge* by Taylor Mac. She created the role of Philomena Moosetail in *The Rez Sisters*, Aunt Shadie in *The Unnatural and Accidental Women* by Marie Clements, Martha in *The Buz'Gem Blues* by Drew Hayden Taylor, and Spirit Woman in BONES: *An Aboriginal Dance Opera*. She has created the one-woman shows *Hot 'n' Soft I* and *II*, *Trail of the Otter*, and, most recently, *Red Mother*.

Muriel recently returned from Norway where she facilitated a three-week workshop with first-year acting students at the Norwegian Theatre Academy. She teaches Indigenous performance at the Centre for Indigenous Theatre (CIT) and is also the program director for CIT's three-week summer intensive. She was a program director and an instructor of Indigenous performance for the Aboriginal Dance Program at the Banff Centre. She has been profiled in *American Women Stage Directors of the Twentieth Century* and has been awarded an honorary Doctorate of Fine Arts from Miami University in Oxford, Ohio.

INTRODUCTION TO HOT 'N' SOFT
BY SHARON M. DAY

Spiderwoman Theater came to Minneapolis in the mid-1980s and performed several plays at the only feminist theatre in town, At the Foot of the Mountain Theater. Muriel and her sisters, Lisa and Gloria, recruited an ensemble cast of local women of colour and created *Neurotic, Erotic, Exotics*. When I saw the performance it was a story that most resembled my reality next to *For Colored Girls Who Have Considered Suicide/When the Rainbow is Enuf*. It was the beginning of a relationship that has lasted over twenty-five years, and it was from Muriel, Lisa, and Gloria, along with their friend and colleague, director Phylliss Jane Rose, that I learned about theatre and how to work with ensembles. In the end, I learned how to take the stories of the people and create theatrical pieces that resonate in Indigenous communities. I have worked with a Native youth theatre ensemble for twenty-three years for which Muriel has directed and created four of our nine productions.

I remember seeing *Hot 'n' Soft* not long after my own coming-out process as a lesbian/two-spirit woman. This theatrical piece made me nervous the same way Muriel herself made me nervous. Years earlier, my partner and I went to see a Spiderwoman Theater show twice. It was at the second show that Muriel came up to us after the performance and said, "So are you two partners?" Just like that. We were stunned that someone would ask us this question that directly . . . in 1985.

After the shows, we invited Muriel and her sisters to dinner. It was over the course of many meals that we learned of Muriel's coming-out process in Amsterdam. She says her sisters went to London, leaving her there, and she met this woman. And that was that. Her sisters Liz and Gloria told me their version of the story: "We were in Amsterdam and we went to London for ten days. We left Muriel in Amsterdam. When we came back, Muriel was a lesbian!"

I think *Hot 'n' Soft* was the first lesbian theatre that depicted the rawness of desire between two women. This is what made me nervous. It was a bold statement when it was first conceived in its erotica and it still has a boldness that few lesbian pieces have to this day. It was also humorous in that quirky Indigenous kind of way. Coyote is portrayed as a feminine trickster similar to the way Beth Brant portrayed the trickster in *Mohawk Trail*, "Coyote Learns a New Trick." It is funny because Coyote tricks herself. Who cannot relate to this story as lesbians when our straight girlfriends from our teenage years wonder why we didn't make a pass at them? The piece on body hair is also funny because we always wonder about the "other." Indigenous people have little body hair or facial hair. I love the way she describes her lover's leg hair as a slippery seal covered with fur. And then when her lover shaves it off . . . the agony of it all! *Hot 'n' Soft* is dynamic, physically demanding, and comes at a brisk pace, and I can't imagine any other woman than Muriel Miguel pulling it off so successfully.

Hot 'n' Soft premiered and was first produced by Buddies in Bad Times Theatre as part of the Queer Culture Festival in 1991. The play was written, directed, and performed by Muriel Miguel, with set and costume design by Soni Moreno and stage management by Deborah Ratelle.

The play went on to tour across North America, performing at Theater Rhinoceros, San Francisco, in 1991; Out North Theater, Anchorage, in 1993; the Indian Summer Festival at the American Indian Community House, New York City, in 1994; the Women's Studies Conference at Skidmore College, Saratoga Springs, New York, in 1996; the Out on the Edge Festival at the Theater Offensive, Boston; and at Teatro Berdache, Calgary, in 2001.

A large, layered colourful quilt of multicoloured and patterned squares/rectangles of different sizes decorated with lace and brocade hangs as a backdrop. The stage is bare; the theatre is dark. MURIEL *starts to moan as the light slowly increases.* MURIEL *is dressed in a white men's tuxedo jacket and soft royal blue pants. She moves to centre stage, increasing her volume, standing in profile.* MURIEL *moves her head forward and then let's it fall back while her hands grasp her legs, her knees bent while her hips gyrate. The movement and voice increases with intensity throughout the opening.*

MURIEL: *(low voice in the dark)* Ooh, ooh, ooh . . . .
(sexy voice) Sounds from the dark.
Woo, woo, woo . . . .
Sounds from the daylight.
Woo, woo, woo . . . .
Sounds from the hall.
Woo, woo, woo . . . .
Sounds from the floor.
Wooo . . . .

Two beats.

Remember when I could hardly wait to get my hands on her.
Woo, woo, woo . . . .
Doorbell rings.
Ah, ah, ah . . . .
Run to the door.
Woo, woo . . . .
Try to get the pieces of clothing off of her.
Woo, woo, woo . . . .
Dissolve to the floor.
Woo, woo, woo . . . .

Sounds from the floor.
Woo, woo, woo . . . .
Bed, bed, gotta get to the bed. *(points)*
Ah, ah . . . . woo, woo . . . .
Up, up, up, up . . . .
Bed, bed, bed . . . .
Sounds from the bed.
Woo, woo, woo . . . .

MURIEL *turns towards the audience, and becomes the angry neighbour.*

Bang, bang, will you two shut up.
Aah, aah, woo, woo . . . .
Somebody's listening, somebody's listening.
AAH, AAH . . . .
Somebody's listening, somebody's listening.
AAH, AAAAAAHHHHH . . . .

Orgasm—a big verbal climax. Suddenly she turns to the audience, smiles, and speaks in her everyday voice.

Hi, my name is Muriel. I'm a storyteller. The first story I want to tell you is what I call first encounter. I have a group called Spiderwoman Theater and in that group I have my two sisters. Now the background behind this is that Spiderwoman was in Europe—some of us had to go to Holland and some of us had to go to England. The funny thing about this is that my two sisters went to England for two weeks and this is the way they tell it:

She changes voice, shrugs her shoulders, and sticks her arms out with a surprised face.

"We went to England for two weeks and when we got back, Muriel was a *lesbian*."

Miracles! So, this is my version of the same story.

She walks in a circle and ends at upstage left.

I opened the door.

She's really attracted to this woman—uses her sexy voice.

Oh, hi, hello.

Extends her hand for a handshake.

Nice to meet you.

Steps back and looks at her.

Oh, you're with her.

She walks to centre stage and lies on the floor, halfway braced by one arm.

I'm tired; I'm going to bed. It's all right, you can come in. I'm not very tired; you can sit over there.

Her head and eyes slowly follow the woman stage right to stage left while she speaks to herself.

She's really very beautiful. If I look at you will you look at me? If I touch you will you touch me?

(looking down) Does she like me?

(to the woman) A Leo, you know, a lion.

She growls and fluffs her hair.

An actress. *(trying to impress)* Spiderwoman Theater, we're a feminist theatre group.

(to herself) She's really very beautiful. Does she like me?

Her eyes follow the woman leaving stage right.

Hey, where are you going? It's all right, you can stay.

She follows with her head and eyes the woman moving back from stage right and then all the way back to stage left.

Are you stoned, or drunk?

Beat.

Oh, both. Yeah, I'll smoke. I'll just lie here *(lies all the way down)* and we can talk.

She moves on her back into a suggestive pose.

Hey, where are you going? *(sits up)* It's all right, you can stay.

Eyes follows the woman moving to stage right.

Look at me. Do you like me? Hey, where are you going?

Eyes follows the woman moving to stage left.

It's all right, you can stay. Oh, you're leaving?

(to herself) Well at least I'll get a good-night kiss from this. She can't refuse that. I'll just pucker my lips.

She crawls downstage on her knees, reaches her arms up, and puckers her lips to be kissed and ends up with a handshake instead. Shocked, she extends her hand for the handshake.

Good night.

MURIEL *stands and speaks directly to the audience.*

Well, I did end up kissing her two weeks later. What I really liked about her was she was so hairy. I was really impressed with all that hair. I'm

Native and no one in my family has hair. What you see on my head is what I've got. So, I naturally assumed most women did not have hair on their bodies, especially down there. Imagine my surprise the first time I ever touched or kissed a woman with hair on her body. I went into spasms of delight. She had hair on her arms, hair on her legs, hair on her back, on her *(yells)* nipples, and a lion's mane between her legs.

MURIEL *grabs her crotch and then starts jumping up and down with the next line.*

I went POW, POW, POW–hair madness . . . . I love hair on a woman's body. I love the feel of it between my fingers *(rubs fingers together)*, I love the feel of it between my toes, between my teeth. What do you think about that? I love the sound of it rubbing on my back, my belly, *(yells)* my forehead. Taste—like salty almonds. I will follow you anywhere if you have hair. I love hair on a woman's body: straight hair, curly hair, black hair, brown hair, kinky hair—I LOVE HAIR!

Now my lover did not love all that hair on her body. Now, how do you reassure a hairy person that you love their hair and you're standing there hairless? Do you think they believe you? No. So, we were having a bubble bath. Now I have to tell you about this bathtub. It was heart-shaped, in red tile. Cute, cute, cute . . . it was so cute. We were in the bubble bath. She put her leg up in the air and the soapy water dripped off her leg, making the hair on her leg matte. She looked like a seal. *(really excited)* Oh, the fantasies that went through my head. Up and down in the ocean through waves together. You know, her frolicking and splashing in the waters, cracking clams on her chest, and little round hairless me bobbing along beside her like an avocado, brown not green. I was having so much fun when she announces to me that she was going to shave the hair off her body. *(touches her heart)* I was bereft. I felt like I was losing a thousand little friends.

Beat.

I look at her and . . .

She sings in a fun operatic voice, holding the last note as long as she can while she gestures to all the parts of the body where hair can grow.

HAIR, HAIR, HAIR . . . .

Speaking of hair, I love coyotes; probably because they are so hairy. This is the story about Coyote. In our Native tradition we have creatures called tricksters: Raven, Coyote, Rabbit, Monkey—these are all tricksters. Tricksters are the ones who, when everything is going well—life is wonderful and POW—they come along and whack you in the head. The really nice thing about tricksters is they can change gender—they can cross back and forth. Most of the stories that have been written about tricksters have been written by MEN, which is why most tricksters are male. What a surprise. This is a story about a female Coyote.[1]

She throws her head back and howls and howls and howls for about thirty seconds.

Coyote was bored, bored, bored, bored, bored. There she was walking around in her cave: what to do . . . what to do. Coyote thought of a good trick. She got out her sewing machine and made herself a beautiful outfit . . . brown velvet pants with pegged bottoms, a white ruffled shirt with French cuffs, a bolo tie, and brown cowboy boots. *(physically acts this out)* Then she pushed all her hair into a grey fedora, angled it over

---

1   A special thanks to Beth Brant for allowing me to adapt her short story, "Coyote Learns a New Trick."

one eye. Then she rolled up a couple of smelly towels and put them into her trousers to make it look like she had a big swell.

(to audience) It was a trick, a joke. Now she was ready to go out into the world. Here comes Coyote, "I'm bad, I'm tough."

She walks across the stage trying to get the hang of the towels, continuing to adjust them between her legs again and again.

"I'm bad, I'm tough."

Coyote sort of walked down the road trying to get the hang of these towels.

She walks around, continuously adjusting.

Up in the sky was Hawk just flying around when she spied Coyote staggering around saying, "I'm bad, I'm tough." Hawk nearly fell out of the sky she laughed so hard. She had never seen anything like it. Coyote said that everybody knows that hawks have no sense of humour.

Still adjusting.

She keeps walking along and she meets Rabbit. She went up and said, "Hey, Rabbit." Rabbit muttered, "These creatures are weird—weird, weird, weird." And with that Rabbit hopped off into the woods.

Coyote's plan was not going well. She was getting really depressed this wasn't working. She started to walk in a circle. *(sadly, with head down)* What to do. What to do. Then she thought of Fox. That la-di-da female thought she was so sly and clever.

(to audience) Now Coyote's joke was to fool Fox. To get her to think she was a male. And if it worked she could tell this story for centuries.

She walks to upstage centre.

So, Coyote strutted up to Fox's door; she knocked on the door. Fox opened the door . . .

Beat. Fox looks closely at Coyote.

. . . and her eyes got very large with admiration.

(super sexy whispery voice) Fox, "Oooo, can I help you?"

(acts dumb) Coyote, "I seem to be lost. Can you tell a man like me where I can get a good dinner?"

Fox, "Come on in. I was just fixing a little something." With that Coyote came in the house. Fox took Coyote by the paw and said, "Would you like a bite?" She turned herself around and with her tail high in the air sashayed down the hall.

MURIEL *becomes Fox and pulls out a handkerchief, puts it in her back pocket to make a tail, and walks away.*

(to audience) Coyote didn't think it would be this easy. This was going better than she had planned. She giggled. *(goofy chuckle)*

(turns around) Fox said, "Did you say something?"

She walks around with her tail swaying.

Coyote, "I was just admiring your red fur, mighty pretty."

She playfully touches her hair.

Fox, "Oh, you like it. It's inherited, you know." And with that she turned around and sashayed down into her dining room.

Coyote, "Smells mighty good in here. You must be a fine cook."

Fox laughed, "I've been known to cook up a few things. I have some baked brie and some sourdough bruschetta." She poured Coyote a glass of white wine.

Coyote, "Say, you're a pretty female. Got a man around the house?" Fox looked at Coyote and she started to giggle, and then she laughed and laughed. *(laughs, snorts, laughs louder)*

Fox, "No, there are no men." *(laughing and snorting)* "A few girlfriends that stay over."

Coyote did not understand any of this. Fox gave her a bit more wine and a little more sourdough bread. And they talked about this and that and Coyote kept looking at Fox because she had such a dainty little tongue and hands. And she would take her tail and wrap it around her dainty legs. Well, one thing leads to another like they usually do . . .

Coyote, *(deep voice)* "Well, Fox, how about a little roll in the hay?" *(shy laugh)*

Fox giggled and ruffled her fur and said, "Well, Coyote, I thought you would never ask." And Coyote took Fox by the paw and walked down the hallway to her bedroom with her tail held higher. Fox lay down on the bed and took Coyote's body across her little body and she started to purr. *(purring sounds)* She started to lick Coyote on the neck *(sensual sounds)*, the front of Coyote's cheek . . . Coyote's nose. *(fun sexy sounds, Coyote is enjoying this)*

MURIEL *breaks out of the embrace and speaks directly to the audience.*

Coyote, "Oh, let's let this trick go on a little longer." Fox took her little paws and ran them up and down Coyote's back and such sounds came out of her.

Coyote, "I really like this and I can't imagine anything else sounding like this. I just love the sounds . . . " Then Fox took her dainty leg and put it between Coyote's legs. "I'll just let it go on a little longer. This is good, good, good. I really like this. Oh, maybe I will wait a little bit longer. That tongue and her paw on my back rubbing and petting. Oh, that little tongue . . . and wow, moving her little legs like that and such pretty noises. *(speaks louder)* And her paws feel real good unzipping my pants *(sudden realization)*, going into my pants!"

Fox, "Oh, Coyote! Why don't you take that ridiculous stuffing out of your pants and let's get down to business."

She grabs Coyote and humps her.

Howl. Howl. Howl.

So, after that, I decided I was going to write this show and I was going to do it on erotica. So I decided to do some research. Do you know there isn't much lesbian erotica? Do you know that if there is, it goes something like this . . . Heidi's gay, hooray, hooray, hooray! The choice of words . . . "She took her hand and put it there."

MURIEL reaches out and looks at her hand.

Where there? Anywhere? Who knows? And if they make it—one of them has to die. Now if they make it and live together and they're happy— boom—an automobile accident and they are both dead. So after that, I decided I was going to write my own erotica story. So, I did and called it "Lesbian Love," and now you may want to call it something else, but that's what I named it.

Lights change. MURIEL crosses to upstage centre. She stands with her hand on one side of her head and the other on her hip with her head thrown back, as if she is lying down on a bed.

I was naked. She was naked. We were lying on a big round bed, sucking and rubbing and nuzzling . . . sucking and rubbing and nuzzling . . . sucking and rubbing and nuzzling. She sucked my toe. I painted her toenails and blew on the polish. *(looks at the audience)* She had big feet, size thirteen—BIG feet. She got up and put on her robe and left the room. I thought, "How graceful, and with such big feet." I painted my toenails.

God was I excited. God was I clumsy. I spilled the nail polish all over her fancy sheets. Got up and ran into the bathroom, got the nail-polish remover and cleaned the sheets. Now the whole room smelled like nail-polish remover. Got up, opened the window.

God was I excited.

Beat.

God was I cold.

She starts acting like James Bond.

I shrugged my naked body into my second-hand grey Armani jacket. I curled up onto the green velvet overstuffed chair. I felt in my pocket for my gold-cork-tipped brown Shermans and lit one with my turquoise-and-silver-covered Bic.

God was I excited. God was I bored. I was both, excited and bored. She came in with two steaming mugs of coffee on a silver tray. She also had bread and butter and a big white bowl with big red, ripe strawberries. She put the tray on the bed. She took a strawberry and put it in her mouth, bit into it, and the juice made her fingertips red. She came to me and put a strawberry into my mouth and kissed me.

Two beats.

The goddamn telephone rang. She answered it eagerly, giggling into the mouthpiece. *(whispering)* God was I excited. God was I jealous.

I kissed her on the cheek. I kissed her neck. I pinched her ass. I slowly slipped out of my second-hand grey Armani jacket. She watched me. I lay down on the bed. I watched her.

MURIEL *opens legs and looks at the woman.*

She hung up the phone, ran across the room, and leapt on top of me. She grabbed my wrists. *(arms up)* She was trying to kiss me. I kept turning my head.

Hopping up and down, shaking her head back and forth.

No, no, no, no, no. She bit me on the neck and laughed teasingly. I quickly rolled her over, knocking the coffee off the bed and rolling her into the bread and butter. I slowly rubbed butter onto her hard brown nipples.

Getting progressively louder and more urgent.

She tried to get up—I pushed her down. She tried to get up—I pushed her down. More butter. She tried to get up—I pushed her down. She tried to get up—I pushed her down. More butter. She tried to get up—I pushed her down. She tried to get up—I pushed her down. More butter.

Long pause.

I slowly licked the butter off her brown nipples.

She sticks tongue out and begins to lick.

The goddamn doorbell rang. God was I excited. God was I naked. She gave me a robe. It was white, heavy-satin brocade with pink lapels. It fell in folds to the floor and swirled around my feet. I sat in the green velvet overstuffed chair.

God was I excited. God was I jealous. I lit a gold-cork-tipped brown Sherman with my silver-and-turquoise-covered Bic. In came a very short woman wearing a brown derby hat.

She mimes putting out the cigarette while checking out this woman.

God was I excited. The short woman was very nervous. I went to her and took her into my arms, pulled back her head, and kissed her. I crushed her to my breast. I pulled back her head, kissed her, and crushed her to my breast. I pulled back her head, kissed her, and crushed her to my breast. I pulled back her head, kissed her, and crushed her to my breast. I slowly put my tongue deep into her mouth.

MURIEL kisses and licks the palm of her hand in a noisy, passionate way.

I picked her up. I put her down and said, "There."

She wipes her hands and walks away.

MURIEL *walks to stage left, turns, and watches the woman coming in again.*

She came in this time with pears and yogourt. The short woman would not sit down. I grabbed her and sat her on my lap. *(put out knee)*

(She points at the woman.) She was pouring yogourt into a bowl.

She came to me and s-l-o-w-l-y squished the yogurt on my head. *(touches head)* God was I excited.

(to audience) If you want to know the rest, you have to do it yourself at home.

Don'tcha just love it? I can't help it. I just love women. I can't help it. I just love them. I admire them. I like them. I adore them. I breast them. I behind them. I thigh them. I flesh them. I *amour* them. *Amora, amorae, amoranum, amoratat* tat tat. Anyway, I dig them.

She creates an opening in the quilt backdrop by draping some of the material over a chair.

Sometimes they can really fool you. Once upon a time, a long, long, long, long, long . . . . time ago, I was caught.

She makes a fist and hits her chest.

She was an average woman. She had pale skin, high cheekbones, pale eyes, pale reddish hair.

MURIEL sits in a chair and takes off her pants, but keeps her black leggings on.

She had an average round body, average round behind, with round average breasts and BIG round nipples.

She demonstrates with a hand motion.

Maybe she wasn't so average.

One thing I knew, she WANTED ME. She wanted my body. She sent me marzipan fruit: pink and purple anemones.

She walks through the opening and speaks from behind the backdrop.

She'd ask my advice on her little problems. She'd get me involved.

She sticks her head out from an opening in the quilt.

Caught—I was caught. And I didn't even know it. She would cry on my breast like a butterfly. She wept little butterfly tears. She wanted me. I didn't know it. I was caught. To tell the truth, I wasn't that interested. I was flirting. But she wanted me. She was so helpless—it was amazing.

MURIEL peers out from backdrop, stage left.

She would just stand there—so open—the goddess.

The promise.

MURIEL pushes parts of the backdrop from behind repeatedly.

I felt like a beautiful damselfly flitting from blossom to blossom. I could smell her perfume. I was caught.

With a choke in her voice.

Caught. Caught. Caught in that sticky nectar she oozed.

Her hands reach through the backdrop.

Her little hands reached out to me. Those sharp little nails touched my body. She was after me. She wanted me. I stopped running.

Her hands create a time-out sign.

It was all a trick. She ran right past. Caught. As soon as I relaxed with lightning speed, hapless me was trapped. Caught.

Her head peers out through the backdrop.

I was caught. *(in a high voice)* "Well to tell you the truth, I'm really not ready for a relationship right now. I'm really not attracted to you." Caught—I was caught. I was so busy sniffing and snapping at her heels, I didn't see the side of the trap closing over me. Caught—I was caught.

MURIEL enters from behind the backdrop, dressed in a high-cut brocade and velvet jacket, sits in the chair, her back to audience, and reaches out her arm.

She sucked the juices from me. Damn it, you're my Venus, you're my Venus flytrap.

MURIEL *does a wild sexual dance with the chair to the entire song* "Venus" *by Bananarama. She is fucking the chair by putting her hand in the space between the back and the seat. She humps and licks the chair all over. She hops up and down on the chair, grinds on it, pulls the chair between her legs, and sits on it.*

Once finished, she drinks some water and cools herself down with a pink fan.

Do you know how hard it is to fuck a chair? Fifty-four years old and fucking a chair.

Pause.

Do you like my fan? It's from a pink eagle. *(laughs)* An acquaintance of mine said, "You're so organic. You talk about rabbits, coyotes, hair, yogourt—could it be because you're Native?" And I said, "Could be." Which reminds me of a story.

A long, long, long, long time ago, but not as long as before there was Coyote. Now, I must tell you about Coyote. Coyote had two girlfriends. One was tall and lived in Brooklyn. One was short and lived in Staten Island. Now, Coyote doesn't lie, she always tells the truth, always up front, straight from the shoulder. She didn't really mean to have two girlfriends. You know how that happens.

Now, the tall one she had for a long time. But what happened is, she went to a dance in Staten Island and met the short one. The short one asked her to dance. She danced with her. She went home with her—it's so difficult. So, she stayed a couple of days at the short one's house in Staten Island, got a little antsy, you know, decided that she had to go home. She called up the tall one, said, "How're ya' doin'?" She said, "Oh, fine."

Coyote said, "Do you want me to come over?" The tall one said, "Oh, yes, come over." She went over there, had a great time. Got a little antsy again. Went back home, called up the short one, "How ya' doin'?" This went on for a while, half-hour here, an hour there, a couple of days here, a couple of days there. This went on for a year. Coyote was having a great time. Then the short one said *(high breathy voice)*, "Coyote, wouldn't it be wonderful if we could spend the rest of our lives together?" And Coyote said, "How about two weeks?"

"I would love it," Coyote said, "I'll be right back." Went home to her house, packed up a bag, called up the tall one in Brooklyn. Again, I must tell you, Coyote NEVER lies; she always tells the truth, straight from the shoulder. Went to her girlfriend's house in Brooklyn and said, "Listen, I have to go away for two weeks on tour. Don't call me, I'll call you. No, you can't write to me." Went over to the short one's house in Staten Island.

> MURIEL lies across the chair and drapes one leg over the back of the chair while the other leg is stretched out—pulsing throughout the rest of the piece. She holds the back of the chair with one arm as Coyote, arching her back and turning her head to the side to speak to the short one or the tall one. The short one and the tall one always arch their back and neck while talking to Coyote.

They had a great time; the short one did everything for her. They were out on the porch, drinking margaritas, looking at the Statue of Liberty and the Brooklyn Bridge, it was just so romantic. Did this for two weeks, absolutely loved it. After two weeks, Coyote got antsy, went back to her house, really wondering what the tall one was doing. Called up the tall one, asked the tall one, "You been fooling around on me?" The tall one was very annoyed. "No, Coyote, I've been waiting for you for the last two weeks, and when are you coming over?" "Be right there." Got there, had a great time. Tall one said, "Coyote, wouldn't it just be wonderful if we could spend all our time together?" Coyote said (bumbling voice), "How about two weeks?" She said yes. "Okay. I'll be right back." Went home. Called up the short one. Again, Coyote was on top of it. Coyote never lies, she always tells the truth, straight from the shoulder. Of course the short one was younger, a little more manageable. Coyote said, "Look, I have to go away on tour for two weeks. Don't call me, I'll call you. No, you can't write to me." Went home, didn't even have to unpack her bag. Went to the tall one's house—spent two weeks, had a great time. The tall one did everything for her. She drank white wine out on the sun porch looking out over the water at the Statue of Liberty and the Brooklyn Bridge from a different angle. After the two weeks were over, got a little antsy . . . Went back to her house, called up the short one, went over there for two days. Got a little antsy. Called up the tall one, two days here, a week there, tall one, back home, short one, back home. Coyote was getting tired.

Now the tall one was getting a little suspicious. The tall one did not like what was going on. "Coyote, we have to talk. Let's meet at a restaurant." You all know what that means. And she picked this restaurant, a really nice restaurant. It was like a captain's table, glass fishing floats, nets. Coyote had three tiers of oysters and the tall one had king crab . . . queen crab! And they were eating and drinking white wine, it was great. Then Coyote looked up, and walking past the window and into the restaurant is the short one. Coyote ducked out another door and said, "I have to put money in the meter." Went out to the corner, got herself together, turned around, came back, looked up, saw the short one, waved, and said (inhaling), "What a coincidence." Sat with the short one, the short one ordered fried octopus. Coyote ordered white wine; they were having a great time and talking and getting cozy.

Now the waitress was watching all of this: one over here and that one over there. Finally, she went up to Coyote and said, "Do you want me to bring your plate from over there?" The short one looked up, saw the tall one, and they both waved and smiled. The short one said, "Come over. There's room at this table for all of us." Well, they had a great time talking, the tall one and the short one. They acted like they knew each other forever. They talked about all kinds of things—music, theatre, poetry, politics, they had friends of friends of friends, they almost went to the same school. Coyote was getting very nervous. *(bumbling voice)* "How about a little garlic bread, a little white wine?" They just ignored her. She was sitting there getting pissed off. She started to pout. They still ignored her. Finally, the tall one said, "I have to go to the ladies' room," and she got up and left. The short one said, "Oh, me too." And she went to the ladies' room.

Five beats.

Coyote waited and waited and waited and finally decided to go into the ladies' room. She got up and went into the ladies' room and there written on the mirror in lipstick it said, "Dear Coyote, eat your tail, the two of us!"

MURIEL *gets up from the chair and stands.*

It's a true story. You know they're still together. Ten years. I know about long relationships. I was in one for ten years. We broke up. Boy was I scared. I was so sad. I realized that I lost my girlish figure; actually, my girlish figure fell around my ankles. I was so afraid that people would see my ankles. I developed a nervous tic. For instance, I'd go to a dance and there would be a woman that I'd been looking at for a long time. I liked her and I knew she liked me and I'd get really excited and say, "Isn't this wonderful," and leave. Nervous tic. Next dance, same thing. Nervous tic. Next dance, ooh, ahh. Nervous tic. Kiss her on the check and neurotic tic, next dance, same thing.

This went on for a long time. Finally, I met this woman. She was really nice. She would drive me all over town, go out for dinner, and, of course, another neurotic tic. It would go like this . . . After having a nice time with her, she would park the car, "Thank you for a lovely evening," and I would kiss her on the cheek, then I would turn, run up the stairs into my apartment in two seconds flat. Olympic champion. Next time, same thing, neurotic tic. She didn't even know it was happening—neurotic tic. Finally, we were at dinner one night and I believe we were having sweet-and-sour vegetable balls. She looked at me and said, "Do you want to come home with me tonight?" And I looked at her and I went *(really scared—screams for thirty seconds)* AAAHHHH, and she repeated the question—AAAHHH—and this time I was feeling her all over. And I went home with her. I was very quiet on the way home.

Silently walking across the stage.

Not a great idea. She lit candles. Oh, good, she can't see my ankles. I took off my clothes, got into bed, pulled the covers over my neck. Cold feet. I shouldn't have done this. No, no, no, I want to go home. Meanwhile, she's billing and cooing at my shoulder. This is a big mistake—no, no, no, big mistake. This is a big mistake—no, no, no, big mistake. This is a big mistake—no, no, no, big mistake. I'm not letting her in. I won't let the woman into her own bed. Suddenly she says to me *(in a quiet voice)*, "You are the sun, I am a flower." Well, the hell with those ankles. *(grabs her)* And we rolled on the bed *(turns in circles)*, down the hall, we rolled into the kitchen, we rolled into the bathroom . . .

She's rolling on the floor, half under the backdrop, and then holding onto the backdrop with her arms and legs.

. . . into the cellar. It was wonderful. What made me think I wouldn't miss it?

MURIEL peeks out from under the backdrop, crawls on her stomach to centre stage, and then comes up onto her knees.

Oh, well, I'm happy, she's happy. I'm satisfied. She's satisfied. She can do anything she wants with me as long as she licks me under the armpits. Howl. Howl. Howl!!

She raises her arms up, throws her head back.

Blackout.

TAXONOMY OF THE EUROPEAN MALE
SÉANCE
JUSTICE OF THE PIECE
BY KENT MONKMAN

Kent Monkman is an artist of Cree ancestry who works with a variety of mediums, including painting, film/video, performance, and installation. He has had solo exhibitions at numerous Canadian museums including the Montreal Museum of Fine Art, the Museum of Contemporary Canadian Art in Toronto, the Winnipeg Art Gallery, and the Art Gallery of Hamilton. He has participated in various international group exhibitions including the American West at Compton Verney in Warwickshire, England; Remember Humanity at Witte de With, Rotterdam; the 2010 Sydney Biennale; My Winnipeg at Maison Rouge, Paris; and Oh Canada! at MASS MOCA.

Monkman has created site-specific performances at the McMichael Canadian Art Collection, the Royal Ontario Museum, the Smithsonian's National Museum of the American Indian, and at Compton Verney, and has also made Super 8–film versions of these performances that he calls *Colonial Art Space Interventions*. His award-winning short film and video works have been screened at various national and international festivals, including the 2007 and 2008 Berlinale, and the 2007 Toronto International Film Festival.

His work is represented in numerous public and private collections, including the National Gallery of Canada, the Montreal Museum of Fine Arts, Museum London, the Glenbow Museum, the Museum of Contemporary Canadian Art, the Mackenzie Art Gallery, the Art Gallery of Ontario, the Smithsonian's National Museum of the American Indian, and the Vancouver Art Gallery. He is represented by Pierre-François Ouellette Art Contemporain in Montreal and Toronto, Galerie Florent Tosin in Berlin, and Trépanier Baer in Calgary.

SPIRITS OF MISCHIEF AND SELF-INVENTION:
KENT MONKMAN'S PERFORMANCES
BY RICHARD WILLIAM HILL

It is my job to introduce you to Kent Monkman, performer, and prepare you to read three of his scripts. But where will we find him and who will he be when we do? Perhaps you know him through his drag persona, Miss Chief Eagle Testickle, a fabulous diva? Or as the painter of travestied Hudson River landscape paintings, in which explicit homoerotic encounters between cowboys and Indians are staged? In fact, Monkman's artistic project travels promiscuously across a variety of media and dis ciplines, including performance, painting, sculpture, installation, film, video, and photography. In many cases this traffic leaves boundaries blurred, the artist's paintbrush or the performer's mascara leaving streaky traces from one to the other as he goes. If we seek his essence we will only catch a glimpse out of the corner of our eye of the spirits of mischief and self-invention. In his practice we see characters from performances become the subjects of paintings, or even the painters of paintings within paintings. Or we find paintings incorporated into installations and performances documented on video. To focus specifically on the aspect of performance is simply to bring into clarity one aspect of a practice that knows few boundaries and in which each component constantly refers to and implicates the others.

To my mind Monkman's artistic project marks a shift in the discourse around Indigenous representation. He is certainly not the first Indigenous performer or artist to address the history of colonial ideology as visualized in the arts, but I think that he is the first to explicitly recognize, respond to, and manipulate the operations of desire at work in those representations. I suspect that his ability to make this move is partly the result of a generational shift and partly licensed by his own queer subjectivity, including the traditions of camp and the performative identity play associated with drag.

Artists of an earlier generation had been so directly traumatized by the history of colonial representation that their impulse had always understandably been one of explicit critique and rejection. Here was a hateful fiction—a web of libels against all Indigenous peoples used to justify every sort of atrocity. It had to be overthrown in order to have any conversation at all. Operating in the wake of this ground-clearing critique, Monkman was able to intervene in a different and perhaps ultimately more subversive way.[2] He recognized that the power of this discourse was its ability to create deep links between desire and colonial politics through the process of ideological fantasy. Like all ideological fantasy it sought to actualize and naturalize itself through representation, with narrative and imagery proliferating in all media. It offered nineteenth- and twentieth-century audiences an opportunity to exercise their desires for masculine power, control, and individual autonomy vicariously through the figures of the frontiersman and the cowboy. These figures turned out to be particularly flexible vehicles for desire, paradoxically capable of both enjoying the lawless freedom and natural beauty of the wilderness and the satisfaction of bringing the lawless

---

2   I believe that artist Terrance Houle has also approached this history of representation as open to subversive, performative, and satirical intervention. See my essay, "A Belly of No Small Significance," *Terrance Houle: GIVN'R*, ed. Anthony Kiendl (Winnipeg & Toronto: Plug In Institute of Contemporary Art & Art Gallery of York University, 2013), 22–29.

frontier into civilized order. Audiences could also project their repressed sexual desires onto imaginary "wild Indians," expressing and condemning these impulses in a single gesture. That these audiences were themselves likely to be fantasizing from positions of relative powerlessness within the confines of the new industrial economies in which they toiled only made these narratives and images that much more potent.

It is as though Monkman saw this vast play of desire and the incredible power it mobilized and said, "Aha, desire. Here is a language I can speak. Images that I can visualize. Characters that I can perform." By giving way to the narrative, visual, and performative pleasures offered—lurid stories; lush, colourful paintings; dramatic, larger-than-life personalities—the artist was able to insert his own fantasies and desires into an existing structure of tremendous power. Happily, this subversive infection is invariably fatal to the objectives of the original ideology. The process is all the more effective because the subjectivities involved—let's call them cowboys and Indians for short—trade in the signs of hyper-masculinity and are therefore always already occupying the territory of gay camp.[3]

The identity play of drag offered Monkman a rich performative tradition on which to draw. Implicit throughout his work is a view of identity as a series of performative acts rather than as an inborn essence. This anti-essentialism becomes an explicit subject in *Justice of the Piece*. In this performance Miss Chief satirizes the essentialism and simplistic identity politics that have emerged in certain strains of Indigenous nationalism, opening up membership in the "Nation of Mischief" to all comers—provided they are willing to be subjected to her satirical critique. As Miss Chief informs us, colonial realities of divide and conquer politics—fighting over limited resources (or, worse yet, casino revenues)

---

3   I have discussed how desire functions in Monkman's work in "Cowboy Justice: an American Trip," *The American West* (Warwickshire, UK: Compton Verney, 2005), 167, and "Too Silent To Be Real," *Expanding Horizons* (Montreal: Montreal Museum of Fine Arts, 2009), 102.

have often obliged our political leadership to think small on the question of identity. But Miss Chief is the agent of a liberated imagination and she is having none of it.

Monkman's role-play slips not only between gender categories but also across ethnicities and racialized identities in a process of satirical symbolic inversion that I once referred to as "drag racing."[4] This strategy is especially apparent in *Taxonomy of the European Male,* a performance in which Miss Chief appropriates the voice of the nineteenth-century painter of Indians, George Catlin, as her own as she dedicates herself to "studying the customs and manners of the European Male." This simple flipping of Catlin's words so that they describe not Indians but Europeans allows us to recognize them immediately as the ludicrous, reductive generalizations that they are. But there is a lot more going on is this gesture of satirical mimesis than first meets the eye. It is, as post-colonial theorist Homi K. Bhabha informs us in his essay "Of Mimicry and Man," the task of colonial authority to compel the colonized subject to mimic their colonizer, removing their difference through a process of assimilation. But Bhabha warns there is a paradox; in a hierarchy premised on difference, *too*-perfect mimicry is a threat, not a comfort, to that order. Thus the colonized subject is expected to perpetually not quite live up to the task of colonial mimesis and "mimicry must continually produce its slippage, its excess, its difference."[5] The result is the production of a colonized subjectivity that is a distorted reflection of the colonizer, creating a destabilizing ambiguity in both identities. In Bhabha's essay the colonized subject is not depicted as an active agent in this process because he sees the results arising from the circumstances themselves

---

4   In "Drag Racing: Dressing Up (and Messing Up) White in Contemporary First Nations Art," FUSE *Magazine* 23.4 (2001), 18–27. I later developed the ideas from this essay into an exhibition: *World Upside Down* (Banff: Walter Phillips Gallery and Banff Centre Press, 2008).
5   Homi K. Bhabha, "Of Mimicry and Man," *The Location of Culture* (London: Routledge, 1994), 86.

rather than an anti-colonial agenda. But Monkman, working at a different stage of the colonial process, is able to use colonial assumptions regarding mimicry quite deliberately against themselves. He can mimic the visual and performative languages of colonial rhetoric with ease; not to show off his successful assimilation, but to create the ultimate destabilizing reflection.

Séance reminds us that Monkman is also a time traveller in conversation with artists of the past who, despite the slight disability of being dead, are still able to speak in the present. In his influential book, *We Have Never Been Modern*, Bruno Latour claims that the "modern constitution"—the ontological consensus of the enlightenment—is based on, among other things, the creation and maintenance of a fundamental boundary between a primitive past and a modern present.[6] Modernity's understanding of time is therefore one in which the present breaks "definitively with the past,"[7] as though time was an "irreversible arrow,"[8] moving in a single direction and "abolishing the past behind it."[9] *Séance* suggests otherwise, demonstrating that Monkman's work is not simply a rewriting of history or a contemporary view of the past, but a recognition of the extent to which we remain interpellated by the ideas, objects, and images of other times. As Latour writes, "[I]t is a long way from a provocative quotation extracted out of a truly finished past to a reprise, repetition or revisiting of a past that has never disappeared."[10] That we need to access this insight through the Victorian Gothic convention of the séance is only fitting. The modern constitution insisted

---

6   For a more detailed discussion of temporality in Monkman's art, see Richard William Hill, "Kent Monkman's Constitutional Amendments: Time and Uncanny Objects," *Interpellations: Three Essays on Kent Monkman*, ed. Michèle Thériault (Montreal: Leonard & Bina Ellen Art Gallery, Concordia University, 2012), 49–83.
7   Bruno Latour, *We Have Never Been Modern*, trans. Catherine Porter (Cambridge, MA: Harvard UP, 1993), 67.
8   Ibid., 69.
9   Ibid., 68.
10   Ibid., 74.

that the continuing agency of the past could only be experienced as an uncanny return of the repressed; that is, as a haunting. In such a transaction, Miss Chief is our happy medium.

I think you'll enjoy your journey with Kent Monkman across the boundaries of time, gender, race, and ethnicity. With such a guide it's bound to be a fabulous trip.

Miss Chief Eagle Testickle, Vaudeville Star
Emergence of a Legend part 2 of 5 (2006)

TAXONOMY OF THE EUROPEAN MALE

Taxonomy of the European Male was performed in 2005 by Kent Monkman at Compton Verney in Warwickshire, UK, as part of the exhibition *The American West*, curated by Jimmie Durham and Richard William Hill.

MISS CHIEF: Upon my arrival here from the continent of North America where I have already passed considerable time in studying the customs and manners of the European Male, I have determined to devote whatever talents and proficiency I possess to the painting of a series of pictures illustrative of the European Male in his native habitat.

The subject is one in which I have felt a deep interest since childhood, having become intimately familiar in my native land with the hundreds of trappers, voyageurs, priests, and farmers who represent the noblest races of Europe.

I have become accustomed to meeting many fine specimens in and around the alleys, parks, and thoroughfares of my native village of Little York.

But alas, in North America the face of the white man is changing: all traces of his former self are being altered through contact with the red man, and those who wish to study the splendour of the European male in his original state must travel far and wide to find him.

Thus, it has become my undertaking to record all manner of his customs and practices before they are obliterated completely, as I trust that my pictures will possess not only an interest for the curious, but also an intrinsic value to the historian.

And so I have set forth on this arduous and perilous undertaking with the determination of reaching every tribe of Europe, and of creating faithful portraits of their handsomest personages, views of their villages, ceremonies, and their sport, etc. I have the opportunity of the free use of nature's undisguised models from which to draw fair conclusions in the sciences of physiognomy and phrenology—with full notes on their character, history, and . . . of course, their anatomy . . .

Now. During my travels I seek to procure various authentic examples of their original costumes and a complete collection of their manufactures and weapons to perpetuate them in a gallery unique for the use and instruction of future ages. This, along with my diaries and paintings will be my great contribution to the study and taxonomy of the European male—a gallery devoted entirely to the bygone splendour and nobility of their glorious European heritage.

The history and customs of such a people, preserved by pictorial illustrations, are themes worthy of the lifetime of one artist, and nothing short of the loss of my life, shall prevent me from knowing them (very very intimately of course) and becoming their historian.

Here with me today I have two specimens representing the noblest tribes of Europe. On piano we have Robin Hood, and Little John of the English nation. They are a well-proportioned people in their limbs, and are quite good-looking, being rather narrow in the hips and rather long in the groin. They are however a little inclined to stoop, as they do not throw the chest out with shoulders back quite as much as the Germans. But, their movement is graceful and quick; and in war and in chase I think they are equal to any of the European tribes.

The English are of fine physique, and their facial characteristics are represented by the semi-lunar outline, the bold and angular nose with clear rounded arc, and a low and receding forehead. They are noble, gentlemanly, and high-minded, although they are often prone to snobbery.

I never romanticize my subjects; I paint each sitter with profound feeling for his dignity and individuality. Man in the simplicity and loftiness of his nature, unrestrained and unfettered by the disguises of art, is surely the most beautiful model for the painter.

From what I have seen so far of these people I feel authorized to say that there is nothing very strange or unaccountable in their character, but that it is a simple one and easy to be learned and understood if the right means be taken to familiarize ourselves with it.

Although their character has its dark spots, there is much to recommend it to the admiration of the enlightened world. And I trust that the audience, who looks at my works with care, will be disposed to join me in the conclusion that the European male in North America is an honest, hospitable, faithful, brave, warlike, cruel, revengeful, relentless—yet honourable, contemplative, and religious being.

I have for many years contemplated the race of the white man who are now spread over these trackless forests and boundless prairies, and I have flown to their rescue, that, phoenix-like, they may rise from the stain on a painter's palette and live forever with me on my canvas.

SÉANCE

Séance was performed on October 19, 2007, by Kent Monkman at the Royal Ontario Museum (ROM) in Toronto, Ontario. Monkman created the piece in response to being censored from the First Peoples Gallery at the ROM during the *Shapeshifters* exhibition. In her conversations with the spirits of nineteenth-century painters Eugène Delacroix, Paul Kane, and George Catlin, Miss Chief's costumes grow increasingly larger and more outlandish as the responses of each successive artist draws more of her ire.

Music cue: opening of "Una vela! Una vela!" from Otello *by Giuseppe Verdi, 1887.* MISS CHIEF *enters in black costume and a small black headdress.*

MISS CHIEF: Good evening, ladies and gentlemen, my name is Miss Chief Eagle Testickle; I am but a simple and humble painter.

Tonight, in the place of my immensely popular lecture on the customs and manners of the European male, I have decided to devote this evening to a discourse on painting, which will occur in the form of a séance.

They say that a great painter never dies. With that in mind, we should have very little difficulty in summoning the spirits of my departed colleagues to this chamber.

I have a few questions prepared for them, and we will attempt to have conversations with three of them here tonight in the form of a casual Q & A.

My first guest for our discussion is one of the greatest painters of all time, the incredible, inimitable Eugène Delacroix. Delacroix was the most important of the French Romantic painters, and it was his passionate brush stroke that influenced future generations like the Impressionists.

It has of course been many years since I have seen Delacroix. While touring as a performer in Catlin's Gallery of the North American Indian, I had the greatest pleasure of modelling for him privately at his studio in Paris. He drew numerous sketches of me, both nude and in my full regalia. Later he incorporated these studies into his famous painting, *The Natchez* as an ode to a "dying race."

Eugène Delacroix, *Astum pey yum'hah Okemow skew* . . . come talk to Miss Chief.

Eugène, are you there, my dear?

EUGÈNE DELACROIX: *Oui*, Miss Chief, *je suis ici.*

MISS CHIEF: *Bon soir, mon cher*, it has been too long, I have missed you dearly, but seeing your great paintings always fills me with such joy.

EUGÈNE DELACROIX: You are as lovely as the first day I saw you performing in Paris with that pushy American George Catlin. What talent you have! And what a beauty you still are!

MISS CHIEF: Why thank you! I think if you're pretty, it doesn't matter how you wear your hair. But tonight we are talking about painting.

EUGÈNE DELACROIX: How I adore painting! The mere memory of certain pictures gives me a thrill that stirs me to the depths of my soul. Painting—and I have said this a hundred times—has advantages that no other art possesses.

MISS CHIEF: Yes, I couldn't agree more! *Mon cher,* how do you go about choosing your subjects?

EUGÈNE DELACROIX: I believe that when one needs a subject it is best to hark back to the classics and choose something there. There are certain books that should never fail, also certain engravings; Dante, Lamartine, Byron, Michelangelo. Poetry is full of riches; I always remember certain passages from Byron, they are an unfailing spur to my imagination.

MISS CHIEF: Monsieur Delacroix, what are your thoughts on colour?

EUGÈNE DELACROIX: Painters who are not colourists practise illumination, not painting. You must consider colour as one of the most essential factors, together with chiaroscuro, proportion, and perspective.

MISS CHIEF: And how do you feel about pictorial licence?

EUGÈNE DELACROIX: The most sublime effects of every master are often the result of pictorial licence; for example, the lack of finish in Rembrandt's work, the exaggeration in Rubens's. Mediocre painters never have sufficient daring—they never get beyond themselves.

MISS CHIEF: Well you are a genius.

EUGÈNE DELACROIX: Thank you, Miss Chief. What moves men of genius, or, rather, what inspires their work is not new ideas but their obsession with the idea that what has already been said is still not enough. The so-called geniuses of the present day are nothing but the ghosts of earlier writers, painters, and musicians.

MISS CHIEF: That is so very true, and we are fortunate to have much of your work as proof of this.

EUGÈNE DELACROIX: The public was certainly more enlightened in periods when great geniuses did not indulge in bombast and bad taste in order to make themselves popular.

MISS CHIEF: I, personally, would never indulge in bombast or bad taste to make myself popular. It was a great pleasure to model for your painting *The Natchez*. What are your thoughts on working from a model?

EUGÈNE DELACROIX: It is a question of effect and of how to obtain it when working from a model or from nature in general.

MISS CHIEF: Ah yes, nature! And what are your thoughts on nature?

EUGÈNE DELACROIX: It clearly matters very little to nature whether man has a mind or not. The proper man is the savage. He is in tune with nature as she really is.

MISS CHIEF: Oh dear! Oh please let's not speak of the noble savage. You know from our former talks in Paris that I find Rousseau tired and boring . . . but you are my guest, so carry on without me briefly if you must . . .

MISS CHIEF exits.

EUGÈNE DELACROIX: No sooner does man sharpen his wits and enlarge his ideas and his manner of expressing them and develop his needs than he finds nature frustrating him at every turn. He has to be continually at war with her, and she on her side does not remain inactive. If man ceases for a moment from his self-imposed task, nature reclaims her rights, invading, undermining, destroying, or disfiguring all his work. She seems to grow impatient at having to tolerate the masterpieces of his imagination and the work of his hands. For what do the

Parthenon, or St. Peter's in Rome, or so many other miracles of art signify to the march of the seasons, or to the courses of the stars, the rivers and the winds? An earthquake or the lava from a volcano can destroy them in the twinkling of an eye; the birds nest in their ruins, and the wild beasts drag the bones of their founders from the open graves. But when he gives rein to the savage instincts that lie at the very root of his nature, does not man himself conspire with the elements to destroy works of beauty? And like the fury that lies in wait for Sisyphus as he rolls his stone up the mountain, does not barbarism return periodically to overthrow and destroy, to bring the night after too bright a day? And this—whatever it may be—that has given up to man an intelligence greater than the beasts, does it not seem to delight in punishing him for possessing it?

What then is the use of so much genius, such great exertions? Does living in tune with nature mean existing in squalor? Must we swim the rivers for want of boats and bridges, live on acorns in the woods, or hunt the deer and buffalo with bows and arrows in order to preserve a stunted existence far less useful than that of an oak tree, which does at least provide shelter and food for other living creatures? Is this what Rousseau meant when he outlawed the arts and sciences on the grounds that they were corrupt? Is everything that derives from man's intelligence a snare, a disaster, or a sign of corruption? But if this is so why does Rousseau not blame the savage for painting and ornamenting his rude bow, or decorating with feathers the apron with which he hides his nakedness? And why should he seek to hide it from his fellow men? Is this not also too elevated a sentiment for such a brute to feel, mere machine that he is for living, sleeping, and digesting?

Music cue: "Sunrise. Daphnis Prostrate At The Grotto Of The Nymphs" from Daphnis et Chloé *by Maurice Ravel, 1912.* MISS CHIEF *re-enters in red costume and a medium-sized headdress.*

MISS CHIEF: Thanks so much, Mr. Delacroix, but we are running short of time and I still have two more guests. Thanks for coming tonight, bye-bye.

EUGÈNE DELACROIX: Ah, okay, Miss Chief, *encore la diva!*

MISS CHIEF: Ladies and gentlemen, the next painter I want to have a chat with is Paul Kane. During the years 1845 through 1848, Toronto artist Paul Kane undertook two journeys across Canada to paint landscapes and scenes of Native Indian life. Calling up Paul Kane should be relatively easy. I can feel his chilly presence behind me here in the First Peoples Gallery, where he resides as diligent sentinel over us First Nations.

Paul Kane, *Astum pey yum'hah Okemow skew* . . . come talk to Miss Chief.

Paul Kane, are you there, my dear?

PAUL KANE: Hello, Miss Chief. I am here.

MISS CHIEF: Hello, Mr. Kane, thanks for coming.

PAUL KANE: So nice to see you, Miss Chief.

MISS CHIEF: Oh really? I always felt that I was invisible to you—not authentic enough to be one of your models.

PAUL KANE: The face of the red man is no longer seen. All traces of his footsteps are fast being obliterated from his once-favourite haunts, and those who would see the aborigines of this country in their original state, or seek to study their native manners and customs, must travel far through the pathless forest to find them.

MISS CHIEF: Oh that's just not true, we're everywhere . . . we're right here, and always have been. But we're getting off topic. Tonight we are talking about painting. Paul Kane, how do you go about choosing your subjects?

PAUL KANE: I determined to devote whatever talents and proficiency I possess to the painting of a series of pictures illustrative of the North American Indians and scenery. The subject was one in which I held a deep interest since boyhood. But the face of the red man is no longer seen.

MISS CHIEF: Ah yes, you did already mention that. What are your thoughts on the model?

PAUL KANE: The principal object in my undertaking was to sketch pictures of the principal chiefs and their original costumes, to illustrate their manners and customs, and to represent the scenery of an almost unknown country. One of the steersmen of our brigade was named Paulet Paul. He was a half-breed, and certainly one of the finest-formed men I ever saw, and when naked, no painter could desire a finer model.

MISS CHIEF: Oooh, I'd like that voyageur to paddle my canoe sometime! Your work is purported to be authoritative in terms of its accurate representations of Aboriginal people. From your own "remarkably authentic" paintings, what would be some of your favourite scenes?

PAUL KANE: The Indians have a great dance called "Medicine Mask Dance."

MISS CHIEF: Oh, this is the painting you have on display in the ICC [Institute for Contemporary Culture] right now.

PAUL KANE: Six or eight of the principal men of the tribe, generally medicine men, adorn themselves with masks cut out of some soft, light wood and with feathers, highly painted and ornamented, with the eyes and mouth ingeniously made to open and shut. In their hands they hold carved rattles, which are shaken in time to a monotonous song or humming noise (for there are no words to it), which is sung by the whole company as they slowly dance round and round in a circle.

MISS CHIEF: Paul Kane, is that story true? Are you familiar with my people, the Swampy Crees, originally from Norway House?

PAUL KANE: The Indians belong to the Mus-ke-go tribe or "Swamp Indians," so called from their inhabiting the low swampy land, which extends the whole way from Norway House to Hudson's Bay.

MISS CHIEF: Yes, that's right.

PAUL KANE: Norway House was supported by the Hudson's Bay Company with the hope of improving the Indians, but, to judge from appearances, with but small success, as they are decidedly the dirtiest Indians I have met with, and the less that is said about their morality the better. This race is rather diminutive in comparison with those who inhabit the plains, probably from their suffering often for want of food, and instances of their being compelled by hunger to eat one another are not uncommon. Their language somewhat resembles the Cree, but it is not so agreeable in sound. The unfortunate craving for intoxicating liquor, which characterizes all the tribes of Indians, and the terrible effects thereby produced upon them, render it a deadly instrument in the hands of designing men.

MISS CHIEF: Oh this is really great stuff, Mr. Kane . . . all right I am sure the audience would be thrilled to hear more of your true stories, but I need a drink.

MISS CHIEF exits.

PAUL KANE: To me the wild woods were not altogether unknown, and the Indians but recalled old friends with whom I has associated in my childhood, and though at the commencement of my travels I possessed neither influence nor means for such undertaking, yet it was with a determined spirit and a light heart that I had made the few preparations which were in my power for my future proceedings. As I mentioned, my principal undertaking was to sketch pictures of the principal chiefs and their original costumes to illustrate their manners and customs and to represent the scenery of an almost unknown country. These paintings, however, would necessarily require explanations and notes, and I accordingly kept a diary of my journey, as being the most easy and familiar form in which I could put such information as I might collect. I trust they will possess not only an interest for the curious but also an intrinsic value to the historian, as they relate not only to that vast tract of country bordering on the great chain of American lakes, the Red River settlement, the valley of Saskatchewan and its boundless prairies, through which it is proposed to lay the great railway connecting the Atlantic and Pacific oceans, through the Rocky Mountains down the Columbia river to Oregon, Puget's Sound, and Vancouver's Island, where the recent gold discoveries in the vicinity have drawn thousands of hardy adventurers to those wild scenes, amongst which I strayed almost alone, and scarcely meeting a white man or hearing the sound of my own language. The illustrations—executed from my sketches, or finished paintings, for the purpose of illustrating the present work—constitute only a few specimens of the different classes of subjects that engaged my pencil during a sojourn of nearly four years among the Indians of the northwest. In that period I executed numerous portraits of chiefs, warriors, and medicine men of the different tribes among whom I sojourned, and also of their wives and daughters. The Indian fishing and hunting scenes, games, dances, and other characteristic customs also occupied my pencil; while I was not forgetful of the interest which justly attaches to the scenery of a new and unexplored country, and especially to such parts of it as were either intimately associated with native legends and traditions, or otherwise specially connected with the native tribes as their favourite fishing or hunting grounds, the locations of their villages, or the burying places of the tribes. A much more extensive series of oil paintings had been executed by me, from my sketches, for George W. Allan Esq. of Moss Park, the liberal patron of Canadian art, and I would gladly indulge the hope that the present work will not prove the sole published fruits of my travels among the Indian tribes of North America, but that it will rather be a mere illustration of the novelty and interest which attach to those rarely explored regions and enable me to publish a much more extensive series of illustrations of the characteristics, habits, and scenery of the country and its occupants.

Music cue: Movement 3 from Symphony No. 4 by Gustav Mahler, 1901. MISS CHIEF *re-enters in pink costume with a huge pink and white headdress.*

MISS CHIEF: Thank you, Paul Kane, for your fascinating insights into the world of painting.

PAUL KANE: It was my pleasure, and please stop by when you are in the neighbourhood so that I may create your likeness.

MISS CHIEF: Yeah, sure. Moving right along . . . Our final guest this evening is none other than George Catlin, nineteenth-century painter who spent eight years living with various tribes of North American Indians.

George Catlin, *Astum pey yum'hah Okemow skew* . . . come talk to Miss Chief.

George, are you there, my darling?

GEORGE CATLIN: Hello, Miss Chief, I am here.

MISS CHIEF: Hello, Mr. Catlin, thanks for coming.

GEORGE CATLIN: I must say that your appearance and beautiful regalia are reminiscent of the personage known and countenanced in every tribe as Indian "beau" or "dandy."

MISS CHIEF: Oh really? How so?

GEORGE CATLIN: Such personages may be seen on every pleasant day, strutting and parading around the villages in the most beautiful and unsoiled dresses. They plume themselves with swan's down and the quills of ducks, with braids and plaits of sweet-scented grass and other harmless and unmeaning ornaments, which have no other merit than they themselves have, that of looking pretty and ornamental.

MISS CHIEF: Oooh, these personages sound lovely, tell us more, Mr. Catlin.

GEORGE CATLIN: These clean and elegant gentlemen are denominated "faint hearts" or "old women" by the whole tribe. They seem to be tolerably well contented with the appellation, together with the celebrity they have acquired amongst the women and children for the beauty and elegance of their personal appearance.

MISS CHIEF: Sounds perfectly civilized, and decidedly less dreary than Mr. Kane's "true" stories. Now, Mr. Catlin, I understand that you have travelled quite extensively through North America painting not only Indians and scenery but also the wild animals of North America such as the buffalo.

GEORGE CATLIN: And what a splendid contemplation, when one imagines the buffalo as they might be seen in the future, preserved in their pristine beauty and wildness, in a *magnificent park*, where the world could also see for ages to come the native Indian in his classic attire, galloping his wild horse, with sinewy bow and shield and lance amid the fleeting herds of elks and buffaloes. That a beautiful and thrilling specimen for America to preserve and hold up to the view of her refined citizens and the world in future ages! A *nation's park*, containing man and beast, in all the wild and freshness of their nature's beauty!

MISS CHIEF: Oh there's a brilliant idea! Do you mean like a Jurassic Park for Indians?

GEORGE CATLIN: I would ask no other monument to my memory, nor any other enrolment of my name amongst the famous dead, than the reputation of having been the founder of such an institution.

MISS CHIEF: Um, well, Mr. Catlin, we'll let that go for a moment. I wanted to ask you about one specific painting, *Dance to the Berdache*. Could you talk a little about this?

GEORGE CATLIN: *Dance to the Berdache* is a very funny and amusing scene, which happens once a year or oftener, as they choose, when a feast is given to the "Berdache," as he is called in French, or "I-coo-coo-a" in the Fox and Sac language, who is a man dressed in woman's clothes, as he is known to be all his life, and for extraordinary privileges which he is known to possess he is driven to the most servile and degrading duties, which he is not allowed to escape; he being the only one of the tribe submitting to this disgraceful degradation is looked upon as medicine and sacred, and a feast is given to him annually.

MISS CHIEF: Oh, could you elaborate on this disgraceful degradation and the servile duties?

GEORGE CATLIN: This is one of the most unaccountable and disgusting customs that I have ever met with in Indian country, and so far as I have been able to learn, belongs to only the Sioux and Sacs and Foxes—perhaps it is practised by other tribes, but I did not meet with it; for further account of it I am constrained to refer the audience to the country where it is practised and where I should wish that it might be extinguished before it be more fully recorded.

MISS CHIEF: Oh, dear. Mr. Catlin, you are a man of curious contradictions, but this is why I find you somewhat interesting. How sad that you have failed in your lofty aspirations to be the founder of a magnificent park where the refined citizens of the world might observe the native Indian in his classic attire, galloping his horse among fleeting herds of elks and buffaloes. For this you may have to visit Germany. However, us beaus, dandies, and faint hearts are still here. You have now also failed to extinguish the dance to the Berdache, as we're about to bring it back, more unaccountable and disgusting than ever. Mr. Catlin, you may now return from whence you came, or you may stay and join in, because it's time to dance to Miss Chief! It's time, it's time!

Music cue: "Dance to Miss Chief" by Byron Wong, 2007, with vocals by Shakura S'Aida, Damon D'Oliveira, and Gail Maurice. Three dancers enter the ring in front of the stage and begin dancing to Miss Chief. The audience joins the dance.

The end.

JUSTICE OF THE PIECE

Justice of the Piece was performed on February 4, 2012, by Kent Monkman at the National Museum of the American Indian in Washington, DC.

A BAILIFF *walks to the mic at the front of the courtroom.*

BAILIFF: Welcome, everybody, my name is Bailiff Johnson. All rise for Her Honour, Miss Chief Eagle Testickle, Justice of the Piece.

A huge overture plays through the sound system as MISS CHIEF *in her long black robe and headdress swans into the room, making a few extra turns in front of the stage before ascending the steps to take her place behind the judge's bench.*

(to the audience) You may be seated.

MISS CHIEF *takes her time adjusting herself, pouring water, checking her makeup, and refreshing her lipstick before addressing the audience.*

MISS CHIEF: Good evening, ladies and gentlemen. Some of you might already know me as the world-famous actress, exotic dancer, filmmaker, painter, and provocateur. I have performed all over Europe—in Paris, London, and Berlin, originally with my first employer, nemesis, and lover, George Catlin. You might be familiar with some of his portraits here in the permanent collection at the Smithsonian. You may also be familiar with my self-portraits, also here in the permanent collection.

Someone cheers and claps.

Thank you!

I am also the chief magistrate, clan mother, CEO, president, chairman of the board, secretary, publicist, spokesmodel, minister of finance, minister of immigration and citizenship, queen, princess, and all-round boss lady for the Nation of Mischief, which holds the vast membership so far of—ONE—yours truly.

And so, I have decided, contrary to the colonial policies and laws of discrimination, racism, and genocide perpetrated by the governments of the United States and Canada—which are designed to shrink the numbers of First Nation, Native American, and Aboriginal people—that I will begin to build a great nation, unbounded by geopolitical borders and blood-quantum laws. The Nation of Mischief.

Today in this court, I will be reviewing applications and hearing testimony from the first group of candidates who wish to join my nation. Following today's proceedings, it is my hope that many more of you may also choose to join.

This court is now in order. Bailiff Johnson, please call forward the first applicant.

The BAILIFF call HANS NEUMANN forward. MISS CHIEF scans through the paperwork.

A German man, Caucasian, in his late thirties to early fifties steps forward.

HANS NEUMANN: Your Honour, my name is Hans Neumann. I come to you to ask for membership because I am, deep in my heart, a Cheyenne warrior.

Monday through Friday my name is Hans Neumann and I live in the former East Germany in the city of Dresden. But on the weekends my name is Sings With Sparrow.

You see, myself and others like me have adopted the customs of the American Indian. I don't do it full-time because most of the year I am a truck driver, but on weekends, mostly in the summer, we all gather to live and dress, or rather undress—a bit like you do—part-time. We like to be completely naked under our loincloths, so we feel natural and authentic like real Indians.

There are over 40,000 others like me in Germany, and many many more in other European countries. They call us hobbyists, but they do not understand—we ARE Native. We have powwows, we sing, we dance, and we dress and live like traditional Native Indian people. It is done with honour and respect. When we are living as Indians, we feel more ourselves—our other lives are the ones that are not real. When I become Sings With Sparrow I am not making fun—I am my true self, and living a life that is more honest.

We learned about the Indian ways from the novels of Karl May, and his character Winnetou. I think you would like Winnetou; he was very handsome and noble. These stories inspired us because many of us feel that modern man has lost touched with nature, and does not live in a good way anymore. Many of us in Europe and the former east have felt very oppressed by our governments. Therefore, we have some understanding of the struggles of the Native Americans.

Our world is so busy, so full of technology, so dirty and polluted. Our politicians corrupt! Everywhere you look someone is trying to sell you something. The Cheyenne outfit that I wear reminds me that there was a time and a people where everyone felt connected. A true sense of . . . humanity.

I ask for membership in your nation because I have tried to join the Cheyenne, the Lakota, the Cherokee, Cree, Plains Cree, Swampy Cree, Ojibwe, Menominee, Sarcee, Blackfoot, Mi'kmaq, Mohawk, Cayuga, Oneida, Onondaga, Chippewa, and even the Metis—but they do not want me. I am hoping that you, Miss Chief, will understand me. I think I could offer a lot. I am a good dancer, and I have my own tipi.

MISS CHIEF: Mr. Hans Neumann, or Sings With Sparrow, first of all, thank you for coming all this way and for your application. I am flattered that you have this profound and deep-seated interest in Native American culture. Indeed, I know the stories of Karl May very well. In fact, I knew Winnetou very, very well. We were intimately involved for a brief period of time, but I left him and moved to Paris to pursue my dancing career in Les Folies Bergères. Of course, you have probably seen my films and/ or read my reviews? I was a star, one of the greatest stars ever to grace the stages of Paris, London, and Berlin.

Now, I have looked over your application carefully and you will be happy to know that it is mostly in order. In Mischief Nation it is true that we rarely wear underwear, or encourage anyone else to do so, with the exception of the occasional raccoon jockstrap, buckskin thong, or low-rise Calvin briefs, but you should stand corrected that it is sometimes the present custom of many other nations like the Lakota, Ojibwe, and the Wendat, and so on, to wear underwear to keep their—ahem—belongings in order.

It is true that you live far, far away from the land of the North American Indian, probably too far to have a clue about real Native peoples and the realities of their everyday lives. But, in the Nation of Mischief, we do not oppose taking a little creative licence, and what is important is what's in your heart.

With this in mind, I hereby grant you full-time status in Mischief Nation.

MISS CHIEF pounds her tomahawk on the desk.

Bailiff, give this man his package. In this package, sir, you will find a hand-signed and numbered certificate of membership. You may sign it and keep it as proof of enrolment to Mischief Nation. Present this certificate for discounts at leading retailers: Louis Vuitton, Hermès, Chanel, and various other luxury brands with which I have lucrative endorsement contracts. Your first annuity of $5 of Miss Chief treaty money is also enclosed.

Next!

The BAILIFF gives HANS his package and calls forward the CUT OUT.

An Indigenous man in his mid-thirties steps forward.

CUT OUT: Hello, Your Honour, Miss Testickle. Please give me membership. I got kicked out of my own tribe because they changed their enrolment requirements. It used to be that our minimum Native blood quantum requirements was one quarter, but the casinos have been doing really well and the tribal council decided that we have too many people on the enrolment to share the pie around into so many small pieces. So now tribal enrolment requires us to have 50% Indian blood or more, and many people have been dumped off the tribal enrolment. I'm a fancy dancer, I've been going to powwows my whole life, and now my band tells me that not only am I not a real Indian, but no longer eligible to live on the reserve or access any other benefits of being an enrolled member. The politics about these issues has split the community and divided families, with many people opposing marriage of non-Natives outside our own tribe. There is so much infighting and debate over who is more Indian that we have lost sight of the fact that we have bought into one of the main strategies of colonialism—divide and conquer!

MISS CHIEF: Indeed, your application has raised an issue that makes my— also mixed—blood boil. Is the glass half full or is it half empty? Here in the USA, the Bureau of Indian Affairs commonly uses a "blood quantum" definition to recognize a person as an American Indian. A Certificate Degree of Indian Blood is issued to tribal members as documentation of tribal membership. The Bureau of Indian Affairs allows federally recognized tribes to determine their minimum blood quantum for this membership—one half, one quarter, an eighth, a sixteenth—based on whatever they decide, they can close membership or disenrol members.

Canada also has a similar identification system for Aboriginal peoples based solely on blood quantum or degree of descent, they just use milder words such as "genealogical proximity," "degree of Indian parentage," "genealogical connection," or "genealogical standard." Despite the fancy terms it's just a modern-day act of racism and forced assimilation.

Article 8 of the United Nations Declaration on the Rights of Indigenous Peoples provides that no Indigenous peoples shall be subjected to forced assimilation or destruction of their culture. Further, the state has the obligation to prevent the loss of such culture and identity.

If we as Native people accept the use of blood quantum to determine our membership we are setting ourselves up for extinction. How can you realistically expect most of us in this day and age to only marry and reproduce with people solely from within their own tribal communities? Most of us now live in cities, and we move freely everywhere as citizens of the world—myself included. Eventually intermarriage will wipe fixed-blood quantum out and therefore Native Americans will cease to exist if we allow our nations to be defined by blood quantum alone. Isn't culture a more realistic way to define ourselves? Why don't WE absorb people into our nations and expand our populations instead—the way we used to do it.

The good news here today is that the Nation of Mischief holds no such blood quantum requirements. It is therefore my judgment that this person be enrolled in the Nation of Mischief!

MISS CHIEF motions to the BAILIFF, who hands the man his package and calls up the next applicant.

A man or woman of Indigenous background of any age steps forward.

ARTIST: Your Honour, I'm a bead artist and I'm struggling to make a living here. I'm a Canadian and I have sold my beadwork all over the world. But now I live in the States and my work is considered "inauthentic" because I cannot prove that I have "Native Indian blood" as required by the US Arts and Crafts Act in order to sell and exhibit my work as a Native American here in the States.

My art was passed down to me through generations of Ojibwe. My grandparents were displaced, and because their band was not recognized by the Canadian government, we can't officially prove ourselves to be Native people to the US government.

My grandparents had almost everything taken away from them, their language, their land, their culture, even the simple fact of being recognized as Indian. But one of the things my grandmother held onto was the tradition of beading. My grandmother taught my mother, and she taught me. But I have no band office from which to issue proof of Native American status. I need a piece of paper in order to be an "authentic," "Indian," or "Native American" to show the US government. Can you help me, Miss Chief?

MISS CHIEF: My dear, indeed, I know your story well. I have heard it many times. As you already know, to exhibit your work legally in the United States, you must be able to prove that you are enrolled in a federally recognized tribe. The Indian Arts and Crafts Act of 1990 (P.L. 101-644) is law that prohibits misrepresentation in marketing of American Indian or Alaska Native arts and crafts products within the United States. It is illegal to offer or display for sale or sell any art or craft product in a manner that falsely suggests it is Indian-produced, an Indian product, or the product of a particular Indian or Indian tribe or Indian arts and crafts organization resident within the United States. An individual can face civil or criminal penalties up to a $250,000 fine or a five-year prison term, or both bla bla bla.

However, as a proud, card-carrying member of the Nation of Mischief, you will be permitted to exhibit your work anywhere you see fit. Based on your testimony here today, I hereby grant you full membership in Mischief Nation.

> MISS CHIEF *nods at the* BAILIFF, *who hands the* ARTIST *their package and calls up the next candidate.*

4. THE HUNTER

> *A man of any non-Indigenous ethnicity in his late twenties or early thirties steps forward.*

HUNTER: Hello and thank you for having me here today. I am a father, a husband, and a citizen of the US of A. I stand before you asking to become a member of your nation as I feel mine has turned its back on me. I used to build houses, and even owned one at one point. But then the mortgage crisis happened and I lost my job and my house. Now I struggle every day to put food on my table to feed my family. The way this nation mismanaged its finances and resources is appalling. As a result I have had to turn back to the land. Hunting and gardening has become my main means of feeding my family, but this nation has stringent restrictions on where, how, and when one can hunt. I need to eat but I cannot break this country's laws as any blemish on my record would put me in the back of the line for any available jobs. I would love to enter your nation, giving me similar Native hunting and fishing rights, the right to put food on the table for my family.

I want to be part of a nation that keeps its hands out of my life, that allows me to be free.

MISS CHIEF: A lot of Native Americans would not feel too sorry for a non-Native hunter like yourself—you're still much better off than the majority of my brothers and sisters in Canada and the US. But Miss Chief is different! I am endlessly generous and sympathetic. I really do want to grow my nation and you're kinda easy on the eyes. I'm willing to grant you entry provided you agree to some private sessions in cultural sensitivity and are committed to learning more about First Nations. As for hunting, membership indeed has its privileges. Once a member of Mischief Nation, you will have the right to fish in my tilapia farm, and we can also discuss your hunting privileges on my free-range, organic, vegan Tofurky ranch.

Freedom is what my nation is all about. Bailiff, give this man his papers! Next!

The BAILIFF hands the HUNTER his package and calls up the next candidate.

5. THE GRANDCHILD

A young woman in her twenties or thirties steps forward. She can appear to be of any ethnicity.

GRANDCHILD: My name is Grey, Your Honour. My grandmother was a Blackfoot. Grey was my grandfather's name. He was a white man. I come from Canada and we have the Indian Act that used to say that any woman who married a non-Native would lose her status, and her children would not be considered Aboriginal. This was not the case for Aboriginal men. In 1985 with Bill C-31, they changed this sexually discriminatory law and Native status was reinstated to Native women who had married non-Natives, including my grandmother. However, my dad married a non-Native, and because I was born before 1985, the law says I have second-generation status, meaning that if I have children with a non-Native they will cease to be Native. That means I'm the end of the line. For my future kids to have status and the treaty entitlements that go with it, I would have to marry a person of 50% or more Native Indian blood. It's hard enough to find a straight (no offence) man who's single, has a job, is relatively unscrewed-up, let alone someone you can actually fall in love with—if it gets limited to 2.3% of the population, I'll be single forever!

MISS CHIEF: In addition to my aggressive and inclusive immigration policies, Mischief Nation needs fertile, open-minded young women like you to bear the children of what is sure to be a great nation. As I have already discussed, the genocidal blood quantum policies of the Canadian and US governments were indeed designed to shrink our First Nations. Our nations did not survive for thousands of years from reproduction alone. We did what you do—it's called immigration. We maintained our numbers by absorbing neighbouring and enemy tribes or white settlers—some may have called it kidnapping. Let's call it aggressive immigration. These captives would replace members of the tribe who had died. They would often be bestowed with some of the same prestige and duties of the relative they were replacing (brother, sister, aunt, uncle, etc.). While the transformation from captive to tribal member was often long and difficult, the captive would eventually become an accepted member of the family and tribe. Ethnic origin—or blood quantum—was of little importance until the federal government became involved.

Now with that in mind, is there anyone else here tonight who wants to be aggressively immigrated into the Nation of Mischief? I have time to capture maybe two more immigrants.

Several people put up their hands. MISS CHIEF points to a young man who comes forward.

6. BLUE EYES

The man is of any ethnicity, in his late twenties or early thirties.

BLUE EYES: Hi. Miss Chief Eagle Testickle. Your Honour. I read about you in the *Washington Blade*, so I decided to come down and see you for myself. While I have been sitting here watching these other applicants, I wrote this.

As you know we have been fighting for gay marriage here in the States.

My partner, Graham, is Native American, a Cherokee, and we were legally married here in DC. His family accepts me, however same-sex marriage is illegal in the Cherokee Nation, and it remains illegal in many other Native American tribes. It's heterosexist that same-sex partners cannot be recognized by their tribes. My best girlfriend is Irish and she married a Chippewa man and is now a member of the band, and of course their children will be too. Graham and I are adopting children and we want to belong to Mischief Nation, a nation that will embrace us for who we are! Please grant my family status.

MISS CHIEF: You have come to the right place. It is sad that our own nations, who once embraced and revered two-spirited people, have become so conservative. I think the most dangerous and insidious part of colonization is the self-hatred from within our own communities.

We existed in every tribe, and our nations had names for us in our own languages, Winkte, Illhama, Agokwe, and so on . . . The French called us the Berdache, which stems from an Arabic word—Bardaj—meaning male concubine. It shows how little they understood of us; we were men and women who from childhood were blessed by the creator with the role of the opposite gender. We were keepers of culture, mediators between the sexes, shamans, or medicine people. We had special roles in ceremonies, and those of us born as males made fabulous wives because we were big and strong. My dear friend We' Wha, a famous Zuni Berdache, was a revered member of her tribe, and was sent as a diplomat to represent her people here in DC. She was a skilled potter. So you see, there is room for you and yours in my nation. Welcome!

Bailiff, give this young man his papers! Anyone else?

A Caucasian woman in her fifties or sixties steps forward.

DREAMER: Hello, Your Honour. I wrote a little something too. It's nice to see you again. Meegwetch for letting me speak. Chi meegwetch!

I'm sure you wouldn't remember me. We met over two hundred years ago. Yes, I have had many past lives, my deepest, most spiritually fulfilling have been the ones where I was a Native person.

You see, I have been able to sort though past-life regression through years of deep hypnotherapy. Through my sessions I began to recover memories of past lives I had completely forgotten about.

My husband went to therapy too and he discovered the same thing! When I was a Huron chief, way before the white man came, I was of course so connected to my spirituality. I understood the world and how it worked, how everything balanced. Sadness was never present in that life. My husband (who was then my mother) had a beautiful relationship with my father—my father then, not my father in this life—and shared a love unmatched by all other lives. In our final years my husband and I would like to live as close to that as possible. We still believe that Native people are so spiritual, and therefore superior. While the creator did not grant me a Native life this time around, I wish to be as close to Native people as I possibly can. Please grant my husband and I membership so we can live the rest of our days in a place where we feel most at home.

MISS CHIEF: It is possible that I met you two hundred years ago, but I meet so many people . . . Fortunately for you, I have decided to begin to merge the Wannabee Tribe into the Nation of Mischief. Normally

Wannabees are rejected by most Native people because we feel like our cultural property is being stolen, and, frankly, it can be annoying. Also, well-intentioned Wannabees usually skate over the harsher realities of our lives and glom onto some kind of *Dances with Wolves* idea of our spirituality. But, having faced discrimination myself, who am I to tell you who you are? I think as long as your heart is in the right place, the Nation of Mischief will welcome you aboard.

Bailiff, give this woman her papers.

In fact, I am going to extend membership to everybody here tonight whose heart is in the right place. Bailiff, you may disperse the membership papers to everyone here who wishes to join my nation. These court proceeding are adjourned!

MISS CHIEF *rises.*

BAILIFF: *(to audience)* All rise!

Cue music—powwow intertribal. MISS CHIEF *walks down through the audience, shaking hands with people on her way out the back of the theatre.*

AGOKWE

BY WAAWAATE FOBISTER

Waawaate is an award-winning actor, playwright, choreographer, dancer, storyteller, and producer. A proud Anishnaabe from Grassy Narrows First Nation, he is a graduate of Humber College's Theatre Performance Program. After the success of *Agokwe*, Waawaate's second play, *Medicine Boy* premiered at Summerworks in 2012. He has performed in numerous plays including, but not limited to, *The Rez Sisters*, *A Very Polite Genocide*, *White Buffalo Cafe Woman*, and *Death of a Chief*, and acted in the television series *The Time Travelers*. He has collaborated with Native Earth Performing Arts, De-bah-jeh-muh-jig Theatre Group, and the Centre for Indigenous Theatre. His most recent projects include the production of his play *Biiwidi-Stanger* as part of the Idle No More Wrecking Ball performance and as a dancer in *I'm Not the Indian You Had in Mind*.

INTRODUCTION TO AGOKWE
BY FALEN JOHNSON

"So are you really gay?" Those words echoed throughout the small Moosonee High School gym as I sat beside Waawaate Fobister, just after a performance of the short play *Savage* by Yvette Nolan. In the script Waawaate played Gary, a young Indigenous two-spirited man who is bullied. Waawaate was quick with his response, "Yes, I am *really* gay," he said loudly and without any hesitation. The boy who asked had a look that began with shock, then confusion, then a smile as he nodded his head in what seemed like agreement or some sort of satisfied approval.

Waawaate comes from Grassy Narrows in northern Ontario, a place not unlike Moosonee, where he probably went to school with a boy much like the one who asked if Waawaate was "really gay." The power of Waawaate's words along with his unabashed claiming of his sexuality resonated with those kids in that gym that day. After the talkback, the kids filed out of the gym, except for one girl who hung back, and after everyone had gone she approached us. She told us that she was gay. She said no one knew and she hadn't told anyone because she was afraid of being bullied. It was heartbreaking but also amazing that she could finally vocalize it. Through storytelling and witnessing Waawaate, she seemed to gain courage, which both amazed and moved me.

Agokwe was based largely on Waawaate's own personal experiences growing up in Grassy Narrows. The voice is so authentic and rich we can't help but be transported. The world is funny and hard and beautiful, and recognizable to so many people. The story overlaps with and speaks to many communities. Yes, it is a two-spirited Indigenous love story, but it is so much more than that. It is about love itself. Love between people, families, and communities. How it is lost, kept, and how it is learned.

Witnessing how the characters transform in *Agokwe* is one of the most compelling parts of the show. The relationship between Jake and his cousin Goose always intrigues me. When I first watched the show I remember feeling the saddest about that relationship thread. The bonds of family run deep and to see them strained or broken was tragic to witness. On the other hand, to see the journey of Betty Moses and her transformation was so beautiful. To see that change can and does happen gives us hope.

One of my favourite moments from *Agokwe* is when Jake says to Mike, "There's no reason for us to be scared anymore." Those words stand out for me. It is a moment of knowing and optimism where decolonization takes place and a traditional understanding is reclaimed. This moment extends beyond the world of the play and gives us a glimpse of our potential future, to what we—and I'm not speaking of just us Indigenous folks—can all understand if we let ourselves acknowledge the land we stand upon and our responsibility to it and its history.

It's impossible to quantify the reach of *Agokwe*—to know who it has touched, who it has taught, and maybe even who it has saved. After two successful national tours with sold-out shows, I imagine it's a lot of people, and I imagine it'll keep reaching even further.

Agokwe premiered at Buddies in Bad Times Theatre, Toronto, on September 23, 2008, from a script developed in Buddies in Bad Times Queer Youth Arts Program. The play featured the following cast and creative team:

Written and performed by Waawaate Fobister

Directed by Ed Roy
Music by Marc Nadjiwan
Lighting design by Kimberly Purtell
Set design by Andy Moro
Costume design by Erika Isteroff
Sound design by Lyon Smith
Stage management by Tracy Lynne Cann

The play went on to win six Dora Mavor Moore Awards for Toronto Theatre in 2009, including Outstanding New Play, Outstanding Production of a Play, Outstanding Direction, Outstanding Performance, Outstanding Costume Design, and Outstanding Lighting Design.

Following its premiere in 2008, *Agokwe* went on tour throughout Canada in 2011, making stops at the Yukon Arts Centre, Whitehorse; the University of Saskatoon Drama Department North Studio, Saskatoon; and at the Vancouver East Cultural Centre, Vancouver.

CHARACTERS

Nanabush
Jake
Mike
Betty Moses
Shyanne

NANABUSH enters during a blackout in a bird half mask and wings. As the lights come up, NANABUSH is partially obscured by fog.

NANABUSH: Hello! Good evening. Can you see me? You can see me, right? Of course you can see me. I am standing right in front of you, flesh and blood. But the only reason you can see me is because I choose for you to see me. Before you came in here *(points to someone in the audience)* I was the shithead who spilled coffee on you at the office. I was the old man with the hugest boner protruding through his pants on the street. A moment ago, I was the itch on the ring of your asshole as you sat down and took your seat. I am Nanabush. I am a trickster. I am the trickster, the trickster of tricksters.

The wings pull away as NANABUSH spins.

So, let's just get straight to the point. I'm here to tell you something; something very important. Once you get it, I want you to act on it and tell your friends, and tell your friends to tell their friends, and tell their friends to tell their friends. That way we can all live together like a nice big happy family. Do you like living in a nice big happy family? I know I do. I mean, who wouldn't want to live in a nice happy family? Some of you are disagreeing with me. Why is that? Maybe your family is disgusting? Maybe every time when your family sits down to have a nice big meal someone always manages to fart, or burp, or choke, or argue until you want to die? Or is it just simply the fact that no one in your family gets along or understands you . . . or whatever the case is, the truth is, not everyone has a nice big happy family. You know why? Because humans are stupid. Stupid, I tell ya—they may be the smartest species on the planet, but they are also the stupidest. Not only that, they're also one of the most disgusting and despicable species around; makes me sick to my stomach. Sorry to give you the bad news but I am just being honest. They—you—yes you, you're gross. You dirty everything. Everything you get your filthy little hands on, it gets dirty—the land, the air, the water, and yourselves. Lost people, it's a shame. But I should give you some credit; you are trying to make things better. Everyone is trying to think green to save the planet, to save yourselves, but its not easy being green, or white, or yellow, or black, or Anishnaabe, red! That's why I am here to tell you about the Anishnaabe, my lost people. Their culture is disappearing, going fast. So many things have changed. So many things have been taken away from them: their land, their traditions, their freedom, and their sense of who they were and who they are. Oh, I know you have heard this all before. Poor Anishnaabe, why don't they just get off the bottle and get over it? I'll tell you why. Because once you've been screwed it's hard to unscrew YOURSELF!! Oh . . . am I making you a little bit uncomfortable? Oh, I know I am not being the apologetic little Indian. Well, I don't give a shit because I am Nanabush. The truth isn't always pretty and it isn't easy. It took two hundred years for an apology and all they have to say is "I'm SOORYYYYYY"!! And what do you want me to say? "Oh oh, Mr. Harper, its okay. I will just go and find my little children's missing bones that're now part of this condo that just got built here." Well, we all know what's been done—man's inhumanity to man, tsk, tsk, tsk . . . like I said, you humans are stupid. All we got is the present and the future so let's make it a fabulous one. Anyway, before you folks showed up, back in the day when you looked around and as far as the eyes could see everything was available to the Anishnaabe. There was greed. There was war. But there was no prejudice against ummm . . . what do you people call them nowadays? Gays? Queers? Fags? Homo?

NANABUSH *laughs.*

Homo, that word cracks me up. There are many words used for two-spirited people in the Indian languages: Ihamana from the Zuni, Gatxan from the Tlingit, Nadleeh the Navajo, Mohave the Alyahas, Winkte the Lakota Sioux, Mexoga the Omaha. Oh I can go on and on and on and on, but my favourite, my absolute favourite of them all, is the Anishnaabe word—Agokwe. Agokwe! Come on, say it with me—Agokwe, Agokwe! I can't hear you! Agokwe! There you go! Doesn't that just feel so amazing coming out of your mouth? Agokwe! Ooohh . . . when I say it I just feel so glam glam! Agokwe! Mmm . . . I love it! It means within the man there is a woman; not one spirit, but two. Two-spirited—isn't that lovely? Yes, there was a time when the Anishnaabe had no prejudice against a boy who was Agokwe. Oh no, it was quite the opposite. The Agokwe men would hold power and represent strength because they had maleness and femaleness totally entwined in one body. They were known to be able to see with the eyes of both man and woman. If they did extraordinary things in their lives that broke with tradition it was assumed they had the spiritual authority and power to do so, therefore they weren't questioned. They were shamans, healers, mediators, and interpreters of dreams whose lives were devoted to the welfare of the group. He would do both men's work and woman's work; he would teach children, chop the wood, make a basket, kill a moose, make clothes, paddle across the great lake, protect the woman and children during war, lead a ceremony . . . he was pretty much the ultimate auntie with high status within the community. Also, if he was single, he would be a much-sought-after wife, because what husband wouldn't want a wife who was beautiful and glamorous and strong as a horse and who could be a hunter *(thrusts pelvis)* and a gatherer *(bends over)* in the bedroom. At social occasions, the Agokwe's dance card would always be full.

Drum music begins.

Starting at a very young age, if the parents noticed their boy child was disinterested in boyish play and manly work, they would set up a ceremony to determine which way the boy would be brought up. Some communities would get the boy to stand in a circle surrounded by his friends and family and they would sing and play the drum for him, and if he danced in the way of a woman, because he could not help himself, they would raise him as an Agokwe.

Drum music ends.

Other communities would put the young boy in a circle of brush, where he would find a man's bow and a woman's basket. They would light the brush on fire and he had to choose one of the items. If he ran out with the basket, he would be raised as an Agokwe. The Anishnaabe knew that in order for there to be a nice big happy family everybody had to have a place. The Anishnaabe didn't waste people. They had enough wisdom to realize that there was enough room for more than two sexes in their world, and so they welcomed every new Agokwe born into their community. But that was the good old days. The story I am about to tell is not about the good old days. It's about right now. It's about two Anishnaabe boys named Jake and Mike. Let me introduce you to Jake.

JAKE: Oh my god! I am so excited for this weekend. It's the All Nations Hockey Tournament in Kenora. This is where all the reserves in the area come together for this huge hockey tournament. I get to see Mike. He is going to be playing in it. He is on the Windigo Bay team. I am going to watch all of his games. It's exciting because my reserve, Red Beaver, and his reserve, Windigo Bay, are the two top teams in the tournament. All my cousins, especially Goose, are going to wonder why I am going to watch Windigo Bay play and not friggin' stinky Red Beaver. The reason is because the guys on my rez are just plain ugly. Greasy hair and pimply boys just gross me out. Well, except for my cousin Powerful Lightning Bolt, but he is my cousin. People just don't go out with their cousins, right? Ewww . . . I can't believe Goose went out with Powerful Lightning Bolt because they actually are cousins. I think they are like third cousins. I know, it's so weird and gross. But he was like, oh well, at least we are third cousins and not second or first cousins because that would be just wrong. That made me so nervous because they were messing in the same gene pool. Can you imagine if she got knocked up? Who knows what their tadpoles would look like? Anyway, I couldn't go out with Powerful Lightning Bolt even if he was gay, and with a name like that, GAWD. That's why I have to go somewhere else to find a boy—like from Windigo Bay. The first time I saw Mike was at the Kenora Shoppers Mall. I remember it like it was yesterday. I had driven into town to buy a new pair of jeans. I was mindin' my own business, making my way to the Warehouse One jeans store when suddenly I got this creepy feeling that someone was watching me. You know that feeling when the hairs on the back of your neck stand on end? I slowly did a glaze-over of the mall and there he was standing opposite of Warehouse One; the most beautiful Ojibwe boy I have ever seen was staring at me and I couldn't help but stare back. He's nice and tall. He had nice, dark, glowing Indian skin. Nice toned-muscle arms. Nice developed chest. Nice hair. Nice eyes. Nice lips. Oooo . . . Nice basket. Just soooooooooooooo nice . . . hmm. It felt like we were staring at each other for eternity, even though I am sure it was only for a few seconds, but in that brief time the heat between us had become so intense I had to look away. When I gathered my courage to look back, he was gone. In that moment I had these emotions, feelings, sensations I had never felt before. Was it love or lust at first sight? I didn't know and I didn't care. All I knew was I had to know everything I could about him. I couldn't tell anybody why. I am not even sure I knew myself. So, I described him to Goose and asked if she knew him, and she did. Of course, she also wanted to know why I was asking about him. I made up some lie that he stole some girl that I was trying to pick up. Although she was pissed off hearing about this she told me his name was Mike. Oh . . . Mike. Mike. Mike. Because of the hockey tournament this weekend there is going to be a lot of parties and huge lineups to get in the bars. I am not really quite old enough, but I have a fake ID. My cousin Goose made me a fake Indian Status Card. It better freakin' work because some assholes don't take status cards. But that doesn't matter. I just can't wait. There are pretty much three bars in Kenora. There is the ghetto Native bar where all the old stinky Natives go . . . and now that I think of it there are some old stinky white people that go there too. Then there is this cool young hip white bar where all the cool whiteys go, which I probably won't go to just because I am not really white enough. That means I am going to go to Milltown, the cool Native bar. There ain't no question in my mind that's where I'm going to go because that's probably the bar where Mike is going to be. (fearful and excited) Eeeeeeeeeeeeeeeeeeeee . . .

NANABUSH *does a drunken whopping sound.*

NANABUSH: During the All Nations Hockey Tournament Kenora turns into a party town. All the whiteys love it but hate it at the same time. They love it because it gives them good business. They hate it because they are scared of the Natives. You know why—because my people can be such wild party animals.

More drunken whopping noises.

It's true. The Anishnaabe always loved to get high, but in the old days they found it naturally. Then booze arrived and my people discovered they loved it and the whiteys loved selling it to them. And to this day it's a love-hate relationship, just like so many unhappy marriages. But some people learn to love themselves enough to leave an unhappy marriage. And that's just what Betty Moses did.

BETTY MOSES INTRO

BETTY MOSES: Hi! Boozhoo! My name is Betty Moses and I'm an alcoholic. I am from the Windigo Bay First Nation. I been an alcoholic for twenty years. I have a teenaged son named Michael. He lives with me on the reserve. I decided a couple years ago that I needed to quit drinking. I went to treatment to go and clean up. Alcohol has really affected me in many ways. It has affected my health, my job, and my trapline. Yes, I have a trapline. It was my ni-dede's, my father's. Ni-dede gave it to me before he died. But, oh jeez, before I started the program I hadn't been there in ten years or so. I missed those good ol' trapping days. I was once the best trapper on my reserve. Yes, I beat all the guys from my reserve. They called me that tough ol' Betty Moses. It was actually the time when I won the contest for best trapper that I had my first drink. Everybody was offering to buy me rounds, and I didn't have any until this big buck, Douglas Big Canoe, slid me a glass of whiskey. He was so handsome, how could I refuse? That's how I met my ex-husband Douglas Big Canoe. We fell in love over a bottle of whiskey and his big canoe. He's Mike's dad and a fucking asshole and a lying piece of shit. The bastard cheated on me and took off and moved in with this younger piece of trash, a little slut, eh? I can give him credit for two things: he got me pregnant with his big canoe and taught Mike how to play hockey.

Oh man, my boy is such a good hockey player. Oh, this weekend is the All Nations Hockey Tournament in Kenora. My son Mike is in it. He is the assistant captain of the hockey team from Windigo Bay. All the girls are always coming over and trying to get together with him. He is popular with dem little sluts. He is too good for them though. He needs to get out of here and go somewhere that has more opportunity. This place is just too small for such big talent. I worry about my Mikey if he stays here. Although he presents a smiling face, I can see this sadness in his eyes and my heart senses there is an emptiness in him, a longing for something I can't give him, and all I wish for is his happiness. For my Mikey I started the program and I went back to my trapline to raise enough money to buy his hockey equipment and to pay for his hockey lessons. That's the only time I see the sparkle in his eyes is when he is playing hockey. He loves winning. That's why we are going to kick everyone's ass, even that cheating faggy-ass team Red Beaver. Oh, that team sometimes makes me so angry. They are just full of cross-checking and boarding. They are just awful. It may be a close race between the two but I think we will come out on top. You know why? I just told you—because my son Mikey is on the team. The hockey tournament is the only big Native event that happens around here. We get all the reserves from the area to come out to Kenora and take it over. You know I kinda like the sound of that. Take over. Take over. It sounds good, eh? But it's only for the weekend. I have to be careful. All my relatives are going to try to get me to drink some booze. I have to stay strong. I want my boy to be proud of me too. That is why I come here today. Just to remind myself that I don't need the booze to keep me happy.

NANABUSH INTRO TO GOOSE

NANABUSH does a dance to the following pre-recorded song.

NANABUSH: Loosey Goosey. Goose is loose, see?
No one messes with the Goose.
Even though she's very loose—see?
She don't take no bull-moose crap—see?
One false move, you'll get a slap—see?
Goose manhandles all her men—see?
She's the gossip in the tipi.
Her sweet tongue is always loose—see?
Uses it more ways than one—see?
She gets bull moose in her bed—see?
Her long beak gives them the goose—see?

GOOSE is in front of a mirror trying on different sleeveless shirts. Every time she doesn't like one she says "ERRRR!"

GOOSE: Shtaaataahaaa . . . we're going to party it up real hard this weekend. Me and my li'l cousin Jakey are getting a hotel room at the Lakeside Inn—holay—just be real pimped out! Neee . . . It's going to be so awesome cuz the hockey tourney is just right across the street. I can't wait to party there. There are going to be so many hot Anishnaabe boys there. Yiyiyii iiii . . . ohhhhh . . . I love me a hot Anishnaabe boy who can play hockey. I don't think I can date someone who doesn't play hockey cuz, I mean, I play hockey. I play the forward position on and off the ice. That's why I need a man; a real man. I think our Anishnaabe men should always be the warrior. Eeeerrrr . . . He has to do something strong and manly like play hockey or hunt or do something powwow—like sing or dance. If I can get a man who can do all three and is good in the sack, then that's it for me. I am going to marry him and have his kids, holaaay. There is this guy I always see at these hockey tournaments, Mike Moses. He is just so fine and a wicked hockey player. I want to meet him this weekend. He can be my warrior. Haaaa . . . Eeerrrr . . .

She laughs.

Onsaaaa . . . but my li'l cousin Jakey doesn't even play hockey and he doesn't even know how to hunt. But he can powwow dance. He is a pretty good Grass dancer. At least that's something. I even tried to get him to play hockey with me when we were little but he just didn't like it. Just wasn't in his blood. Errrrr . . . People always think he's a fag. I kinda questioned it too. Finally I just had to ask him, "Jakey, are you a fag?" and he said "No, why would you ask me that?" "Girls on the rez are interested in you but you don't bite the bait." "Well, I am just shy, that's all." I was so relieved because who wants a fag in their family. Errr . . . gross, especially around here. So I grabbed him by the weenug and said, "Well you are going to have to get over it if you wanna get laid." He just needs to find a girl. He is just young, stupid, and horny and needs someone to teach him how to use his weenug. I am going to hook him up though. There is this girl Shyanne on the rez that is really interested in him. She keeps asking about him. She is very pretty and a little dumb but she has a good heart and that's why I think she is good for my Jakey. Because I want his first time to be special. I think he'll like her. He better. Awww . . . my li'l Jakey is going to get laid for the first time this weekend and I am so excited for him, even though he doesn't even know yet. I am going to make sure everyone knows that he got laid so they can just shut up about him being a fag. Fuck. That just really annoys me sometimes. I am always having to stick up for him. Well I gotta; he is like my li'l brother.

NANABUSH INTRO TO MIKE

NANABUSH: Pump those arms! Pump those legs! Pump that arse! Come on, Mike! You gotta get psyched! You gotta get ready for the big game tonight. You got to get ready for the girls and guys. You gotta look manly for their googly eyes. You're the Indian that's going to go far, a local Native superstar.

MIKE: Here we go, Mike. The big game! You can kill this game. Kill those Beavers. We'll show them. Remember, Windigo can kill beaver any day because beavers are creatures of habit. They always play too hard at the beginning and wear themselves out. That's their weakness. I don't gotta do much at the beginning. Just let them wear themselves out and go in for the kill. That's why you're the hunter; just like mom. The beaver is your prey tonight. Pfffft. That's the difference between you and Douglas Big Canoe. You're the hunter and he's a drunk. If mom wasn't such a good trapper we would have starved. What use is a big canoe when it's sunk at the bottom of a bottle? Useless fucker—me and Mom are better off without you. We'll see who's the man around here. I'm the man. I'm the man. I'm the man. I'm the man. I am the fuckin' man.

He breaks and cries.

Fucking pussy.

NANABUSH INTRODUCES THE HOCKEY GAME

NANABUSH: Welcome, ladies and gentleman, to the evening we have all been waiting for, the gold medal game for the ALL NATIONS HOCKEY TOURNAMENT! Windigo Bay vs. Red Beaver! Wow! This is going to be a hell of a game. So, how are the Indians tonight? We have all nations from the area under one roof. We have the Ojibwes! We have the Crees! We even have the Oji-Crees! This is a beautiful sight. Look at all these brown faces that came to support their fellow Indians. So, who went on the snaggin' trail? Did you find the person you been crushin' on? Did you wave and say hello? Did you give them a wink or blow them a kiss? If you are getting lucky on the trail make sure you use a rubber and wrap your weenug in it. Oh, I have just been given the signal. There are plenty of these fine young hockey players coming out in a matter of minutes. Are you excited? Are you ready? I said, ARE YOU READY? Okay, let the game begin.

The sound of a whistle.

THE HOCKEY GAME

BETTY MOSES: Come on, Windigo Bay! Howsanaa! Wii-ip! Daga! Wii-ip! Wii-ip-sanaa!

JAKE: Come on, Red Beaver. You can do it!

GOOSE: Yes! Beaver, come on!

BETTY MOSES: Windigo Bay! Shoot! Shoot! You were supposed to shoot, you stupid SNOT!!

JAKE: Yeah, come on, Windigo Bay! Windigo Bay!

GOOSE: Hey, what the hell, man? Why the hell you cheering for the Windigos?

JAKE: Oh, I meant to say the Beavers. Go Beavers go!

GOOSE: Oh my god! Look, look, look, there he is. He is so hot, so dreamy. My man! Mike Moses from the mall. Remember? Oh my god!

I'm getting wet just looking at him. Go-go, Mike, go-go! Go-go, Mike, go-go!

BETTY MOSES: Yes, everybody cheer for Mike! Go-go, Mike, go-go! Go-go, Mike, go-go!

GOOSE: Go-go, Mike, go-go! Go-go, Mike, go-go!

JAKE: Go-go, Mike, go-go! Go-go, Mike, go-go!

BETTY MOSES: He's going to score! Yes! Go! Go! Go! Score! We won! Yes! Yeyeyeye! Good job, Mikey! That's my son! Howah, he's good! He is good enough to play on the national Triple A team. He is even good enough for the NHL. Don't you think? Like Jordin Tootoo and Jonathan Cheechoo. Howaaa . . . imagine if he got in the NHL. Imagine the money. Mikey is really something, really special, eh? This place is too small for him.

NANABUSH TALKS TO JAKE

NANABUSH *appears.*

NANABUSH: Wasn't that fun? But the tournament is over and this might be Jakey's last chance to meet Mikey. That Jakey gots to do something more than just whacking off. It's a shame no one told him his ancestors come from the great line of the Bear Clan; courageous in love and war. He's got to pull himself together. Pull yourself together and go for the honey pot, because Goose has the hots for him too. She wanna bang him big time. Let's see, if Mike had the option between Goose and Jakey, who would he choose? Well, if they had to duke it out in the ring, she would definitely kick Jakey's ass. But what would Mike want? Weenug or dakai? Hmmm . . . I think Mikey want it in the ASS. Yup, I think he'd definitely want it in the ASS for sure! Well, what real man wouldn't want a li'l ass play, because I did after all ask GAWD to put man's G spot there.

He laughs.

At first I thought about putting it in the middle of your forehead, but knowing men, with such easy access you wouldn't stop playing with yourselves and you wouldn't get any work done. So, for the sake of progress, I put it in your asshole because I know how much you boys love to hunt for treasure.

NANABUSH laughs. He goes up to an audience member and speaks to them.

I know this may sound weird, but can you put your finger there?

He points to his asshole.

My asshole? Don't be shy. We all have one. Just a li'l bit, please. Just a li'l fun. Or at least just a li'l poke? Or a li'l tap even? Come on, just a little tap. Ooooohh, I like that! That's hot, hot, hot. I like a little slap and tickle from boy or girl, my ass isn't fickle. Haaaa . . . So, Jakey, what are you going to do?

JAKE: Oh my god! The tournament is over, everybody is leaving the arena and I never got the chance to even just say hi to Mike. What are all those girls doing over there? Oh my god, that's Mike, he is signing autographs. Wow! That's a lot of girls, and he can have his pick of any of them. Why am I wasting my time fantasizing about him? He is obviously straight. What's the point?

MIKE: Where do you want me to sign my name? Boob? Okay, which one? Both? Sweet.

He writes his name.

Mike Moses. What about you? All right, bring your boob here.

Writes his name.

There you go. You? And, what's your name? Roxanne Kirkness?

Writes.

Best wishes, Mike. Okay, ladies, it was a pleasure but I have to get to my hotel. Coach is expecting us to get together for a team photo in the lobby in fifteen minutes and I have to go shit, shower, and shave—get ready for the evening. Maybe I will see you ladies at the Milltown.

NANABUSH: Oh, oh, Jakey, Jakey! Forget about the charley horse, turn around. Look who's coming! All you have to do is say hi and smile, no big deal, only one word—two letters—easy peasy.

JAKE: Oh jeez! He is walking this way and he's all by himself.

NANABUSH: Calm down. Even though he's the hottest boy of your dreams, it doesn't mean you can't speak to him. He does shit and fart too, like the rest of you. He's coming, he's coming, getting closer, closer . . . *(deep breath)* . . .

JAKE: Oh shit, I can't!

JAKE freaks out and looks away.

I fucked it up! Shit!

Headphones and DJ *equipment appear and* NANABUSH *plays some poplar tracks. There are sounds of a party in the background.*

NANABUSH: Yo, yo, yo, wassssup! You horny Injuns get your engines started! Vroom vroom. DJ Tricky Tricksta is in da house! WHAAAAAT?!?! We gonna go old skool, yo, back to the drum, yo. Can you feel it? The heartbeat. All you Ojibwes put your hands up! All you Crees put your hands up! Oji-Crees put your hands up! Doesn't matter if you're black, yellow, white, or red, raise your hands and be happy we're alive not dead. What? Doesn't matter if you are tanned or pale. Shake your tail. Shake your tail. Shake your tail. WHAT? Doesn't matter if you are tanned or pale. Shake your tail. Shake your tail. Shake your tail. WHAT?

GOOSE ENTICES SHYANNE AND JAKE

GOOSE: Shaaaataaaaahaaa . . . that DJ was so much fun! Whew! I'm thirsty! I need some beer.

GOOSE *chugs a beer.*

I wonder where Jake is? He is totally missing out! Shyanne, did you see Jakey yet?

SHYANNE: No, I haven't seen him yet.

GOOSE: Damn! He told me he was on his way. He shoulda been here already, ever slow that guy. Hey, Shy, you know he so wants to get wit' you tonight. He told me. I know he doesn't show it. But he is just shy, like you. That's funny that your parents called you Shyanne. Like, how did they know?

Beat.

Right.

Beat.

So, anyway, as I was saying, Jakey has the hots for you but you have to make the first move.

SHYANNE: But what if he rejects me?

GOOSE: Didn't I just tell you that he likes you? Don't be scared. Shyanne, you and him have to get over your shyness or both of you will die virgins. Look at me, I am not shy, that's why I get all the boys. Boys like it when their girls are forward. You know if we Native people were all shy like you then we would've died off long ago. Neeccc . . . but for real, just grab his weenug and point it in the four directions. Errrr . . . I mean you guys keep talking about wanting to lose your virginity and here's your chance, and what better weekend is there to lose it than the tournament of champions? You know I'm right. Did you call Mike yet?

SHYANNE: Oh no, I am sorry, I forgot.

GOOSE: What's wrong with you? You were supposed to call him hours ago. Is this all the thanks I get? This is how you repay me? After all I have done for you?

SHYANNE: Okay. Okay. Hold on. Stop breathing down my neck. Sheesh! I will call him now. Hello, Mike? Where are you? Oh, okay. Are you coming to the party? Yeah? When? Errrr . . . you're gross. Okay. Well you go do what you gotta do and see you when you get here. Okay, bye.

GOOSE: Errr . . . take your finger out of your mouth and tell me what he said.

SHYANNE: He said he is coming real soon. He has to go to his hotel room and wash his sweaty balls first. Ewww . . . I know! But that's what he said.

GOOSE: You should've told him I would've washed them for him.

SHYANNE: Ewww . . . you're just awful. Oh my god! There's Jake! Oh, no, I can't do this, Goose! I am going to go to the washroom.

GOOSE: Don't be stupid! You'll stay a virgin for the rest of your life if you go. Just stay here, act normal, remember he likes you, and just go for it. Jakey! Finally! I lost you after the game. Where the hell did you go?

JAKE: I was waiting for you inside the arena.

GOOSE: Look at my boob. That's Mike's autograph. I had to wrestle my way through a crowd of sluts to get it. Oh, sorry, Jake, remember Shyanne?

JAKE: Yes, how are you?

SHYANNE: I'm good, and yourself?

JAKE: Good.

GOOSE: Good. Well, you're good. He's good. I'm good. We are all good. So, let's just have a good time. Shyanne, go get us some drinks.

SHYANNE: But I'm not thirsty.

GOOSE: Shyanne!

SHYANNE: Okay. Okay. I will be right back.

GOOSE: Jakey, isn't she cute? She's kinda slow but cute, right? You know she really likes you, she told me that she wants to get with you tonight. Why are you looking at me like that? I told you I would hook you up with a chick. So here's your chance. Shyanne is a virgin and she is just as anxious as you are to lose her virginity. You better poontang her tonight. That way everyone will lay off about you being a fag. All the guys will be so jealous because she's a pretty girl—has nice boobs and she actually has an ass. Neeeee . . . Jake, when are you ever going to find another Indian chick with a nice ass? Come on, Jakey, this is your chance. Don't pussy out! Just go for it!

SHYANNE AND JAKE KISS

SHYANNE and JAKE dance to the music. He is still drinking his beer as they dance.

SHYANNE: Oh, I like this song.

JAKE: Me too.

SHYANNE: I think you're so cute. I really like your lips.

JAKE: Thank you. I think you are sexy too.

SHYANNE: Kiss me.

JAKE: In here?

SHYANNE: Yeah, why not?

He drops his cup. They start kissing.

NANABUSH: Shyanne and Jakey sitting in a tree. K-I-S-S-I-N-G. First comes lips, then comes tongue, grab your weenug and have some fun.

SHYANNE: Hmmm . . . you're a good kisser. I didn't expect that. Let's go somewhere private.

NANABUSH: Well, wonders never cease. Looks like Jakey is going to dip his weenug in a little dakai tonight.

JAKE: Oh my god! This is it. I'm about to lose my virginity. With a chick! I always thought it would be with some hot guy with hot abs, hot pecs, and big weenug, or at least a weenug! Oh well . . . she's hot enough . . . boobs are nice . . . good kisser.

JAKE starts talking to his penis.

All right, Billy Bob, wake up! Come on, wake up, Billy—this is our big chance, our time to shine, our big moment. After this, no more being called fag on the rez. Oh, Billy! Don't fail me now! Don't do this! Shit! This isn't working.

SHYANNE is embarrassed and leaves.

No, don't go! I remembered your name. I can get it up. Really, I just need a little more time. Wait!

GOOSE: Hey, Mike. How was the photo shoot?

MIKE: Huh? Oh, oh it was easy, a couple snaps and we were done.

GOOSE: I waited for you at the Milltown. Isn't that where you said you were going to be tonight?

MIKE: Did I? I guess I forgot. Do I know you?

GOOSE: Maybe this will remind you.

She shows him her boob.

MIKE: Sorry, I signed so many boobs I can't remember which boobs belong to whom. If you don't mind me saying, you do have a lovely pair.

GOOSE: Thank you.

MIKE: So, what's your name?

GOOSE: Goose.

MIKE: I love the taste of goose.

GOOSE: Well, lucky me. You know, I thought you were amazing in the game today. You got a girl?

MIKE: No one steady. But I got my eye on a couple of chicks.

GOOSE: Like who?

MIKE: Well, there is Susie Blackhawk and maybe Roxanne Kirkness.

GOOSE: Oh, Susie and Roxie—holay. I know those girls. They're from my rez. They're cute, especially Susie with her long black hair. But I don't know if I should tell you this, I'm not one to gossip, but you should know just in case. The thing about Susie is that she is famous on my reserve for giving all the boys gonorrhea. Shiii . . . I know, I feel terrible saying this, but she is like the community gonorrhea bicycle. Errr . . . and the thing about Roxanne—if you wanna know the reason why she always wears jeans and long skirts it's because she has a prosthetic leg. Onsaaa . . . I am not sure if that bothers you. But this guy took her out on a date a couple months ago and he was feeling her up under her skirt and her leg accidentally came off in his hand. Errr . . . and people could hear him screaming for miles.

MIKE: You sure know how to run interference with your competition.

GOOSE: Oh no, it's not like that. I just thought they were things you might want to know.

MIKE: Well, is there anything about you I should know?

GOOSE: Yeah, I'm terminally horny.

MIKE: Sounds like you need a doctor.

GOOSE: Maybe I just need a good injection. You want to go someplace?

MIKE: I can't, I got to stick around and party with the boys for a little while longer or I will never hear the end of it.

GOOSE: Screw the boys.

MIKE: Isn't that your job?

GOOSE: Ha ha . . . what about meeting me on the beach in an hour?

MIKE: Sounds great.

GOOSE: See you then.

She kisses him.

BETTY MOSES DREAM

NANABUSH: Good evening, Betty! Betty Moses! I just came here to tell you something.

There's going to be a change; something that will change your life forever. There is nothing you can do to stop it. So I want you to be strong. Agokwe . . . Betty . . . Agokwe . . . you know what that means? It means within the man there is a woman . . . not one spirit but two . . . two-spirited, isn't that lovely? Not everything is what it appears to be . . . even things that are close to your heart . . . you see but you do not . . . not one spirit but two . . . ice and fire . . . ice and fire, Betty . . . from your belly to the ice . . . not one spirit but two . . . Agokwe!

BETTY MOSES: Holy jeez! Oh, a dream, it was only a dream. A creature. What was he saying? Ice and fire? Not one spirit but two? Agokwe? Within a man there is a woman? What the hell does that mean?

NANABUSH: Jakey? Jakey? Where did li'l Jakey go? Oh, there he is. Awww . . . crying like a little girl because his weenug let him down. Wandering all alone in the dark like so many of my lost people because they cannot see the light that shines within them. The light that can only shine bright when one is true to oneself. Agokwe, Jakey, Agokwe. It's okay to cry. It takes great strength to cry like a woman, but cry for the right reasons. Self-pity is a waste of time. Come on, girl, man the fuck up. Not one spirit but two, that is the light that shines within you. There is a fire that burns in your heart like another who wanders alone in the dark. The fire will guide you on the wings of a dove. Go to the fire and find your true love.

   The sounds of branches breaking.

MIKE: Hello, is someone there?

JAKE: Sorry. Am I intruding? I was walking in the woods and I saw the fire. Do you want to be alone?

MIKE: Doesn't make any difference to me. Don't I know you?

JAKE: Huh? No, we've never met.

MIKE: You look familiar. I've seen you somewhere before.

JAKE: Maybe at the party.

MIKE: No, not the party, somewhere else, maybe at a powwow? You're a Grass dancer, right?

JAKE: Yeah, that's right.

MIKE: Your colours are blue, white, and red. Your head roach is pretty cool too.

JAKE: Wow. You remember my colours?

MIKE: I remember your white eagle feathers because they are so rare. I also remember seeing you dance. You weren't like any of the other dancers. You had your own style. You were like the grass blowing in the wind. You looked so free, like you didn't have a care in the world.

JAKE: That's how I feel when I'm dancing.

   Beat.

But I always have these intense butterflies floating around in my stomach and I feel like I'm going to puke.

MIKE: That's exactly how I feel every time I am about to play a game. I get those nasty butterflies too.

JAKE: Huh. I would've never guessed because you seem so brave on the ice. By the way, my name is Jake.

MIKE: Mike.

JAKE: Yeah, I know who you are. Everyone knows who you are.

MIKE: They think they know me but they have no idea.

JAKE: I think I know what you mean.

MIKE: You do?

JAKE: Do you go to the Kenora Shoppers Mall often?

Beat.

I think you know what I'm talking about. I saw you. You saw me. And I think we both know who we really are.

MIKE: What the hell are you talking about?

JAKE: I . . . I'm . . . I think we play on the same team. And I'm not talking about hockey.

MIKE: Are you a fag?

JAKE: I don't know what I am but I know you were staring at me at the mall, and I was staring at you. I think we both know what was going on.

Beat.

And if you want to beat the shit out of me right now, go ahead. But I have to tell you, I like you. I don't know why. I don't know how, but I do. I like you. So go ahead, beat the shit out of me; it wouldn't be the first time.

MIKE laughs.

MIKE: And you think I'm the brave one?

JAKE and MIKE kiss.

NANABUSH: Not one spirit but two, that is the light that shines within both of you. In this world twin flames can meet in the dark. When they come together they ignite true love's spark.

JAKE: I can't believe this is finally happening . . . feels good . . . scary.

He looks at MIKE, *who is crying.*

What's wrong? Why are you crying?

MIKE: Fuck! Because I'm scared too. I've been fighting this for so long. Pretending to be somebody—this fake somebody—but too scared to be a real nobody. The first time I really noticed you was at the powwow. I had no idea who you were, but when I saw you I thought you were so beautiful in your regalia and I was confused and pissed off because you made me want something I knew I shouldn't want. But when I saw you dancing I couldn't take my eyes off you, no matter how pissed off I was. After the powwow I tried to put it out of my head, but when I saw you at the Kenora Mall all of those feelings came back and I wanted to punch you in the face to make it stop. But instead I couldn't stop myself from staring at you, and when you looked back I chickened out and took off.

JAKE: There's no reason for us to be scared anymore.

JAKE and MIKE *kiss again.*

GOOSE: Errr . . . What the fuck? You guys are faggots? Two faggots kissing? Mike Moses is a fucking faggot? Ya, you better run off . . . Faggot! I can't believe you, Jake. How could you do this to me? You were supposed to be with Shyanne. I defended you this whole time, you fucking liar. My cousin's a fucking faggot.

JAKE: Shut up! Shut up, Goose! I tried to tell you. I tried to tell you but you wouldn't listen to me and you wouldn't give me a chance.

GOOSE: Fuck you, Jake! You can just fucking rot in hell.

NANABUSH TALKS ABOUT TIME PASSING AND WINDIGO

NANABUSH: Summer, fall, winter, spring, summer . . . one year has passed since that fateful night of Jake and Mike's first kiss. No words were spoken between them since those moments of bliss. Goose abandoned Jake because she felt like a fool. A woman scorned; her heart turned cruel. Heart broken and rejected, Jake went away to school. Time passes slowly when the heart longs for another. Fall, winter, spring, summer . . . there is a constant flow . . . some things wither while other things grow . . . and when a heart grows cruel . . . it gives birth to the Windigo. The Windigo is a spirit that feeds on the weak. Cast off and alone, it is Mike that it seeks. Jakey, listen to the Windigo's howl.

Strobe lights flash throughout the end of the Windigo scene.

It's ravenous. Hungry. It's looking for someone that's close to your heart . . . hunting for Mike, and he'll tear him apart.

Windigo speaks as he makes jerky movements.

WINDIGO: Noondes ski de. Noondes ski de. Noondes ski de. Mikey. Gapinaaskoon. Mikey. Gapinaaskoon. Mikey. Gapinaaskoon. Kiwi amon. Mikey. Kiwi amon. Mikey.

Noondes ski de—I'm hungry.

Gapinaaskoon—I am coming for you.

Kiwi amon—I am going to eat you.

JAKE FINDS OUT MIKE DIES

SHYANNE: Oh, Jake. Oh my goodness. What are you doing here?

JAKE: Sorry, I should have called before I came. I got back home a week ago and I've been looking for Mike. I tried to contact his coach but he wouldn't return my calls. Whenever I've tried to talk to any of Mike's teammates, they've ignored me or slammed the door in my face. I need to know what's going on. Please, Shyanne, you're the only person I can think of who might know where he is.

SHYANNE: Oh, you haven't heard about Mike? I thought you knew. I thought Goose or somebody would have told you. Everything changed since that night. Goose told people about you and Mike. I never believed it . . . but everybody else did. And Mike, he . . . I don't see that Goose anymore because of the things she said about Mike and what happened. Like I said, I never believed it . . . I . . . you were such a good kisser . . . I never believed it.

JAKE: Shyanne, tell me what happened to Mike.

JAKE CONFRONTS GOOSE

GOOSE: Shaataahaa . . . No, that is so funny! What are you doing now? I'm just at the Kenora Shoppers Mall and was thinking of buying a new pair of jeans. Of course they are going to be tight . . . neeee. You want to come and meet me? I'm standing in front of the Warehouse One jean store. Yeah I'll wait, just don't take too long. Oh my god, oh my god, I gotta go; I see my cousin, Jakey. Yeah, he is the one I told you about. No, I don't want him to see me. I don't want to talk to him. I'll call you in a bit and we'll meet somewhere else. I gotta go.

JAKE: Goose!

GOOSE: Shit . . . Jakey, you're back!

JAKE: Yeah, so how are you, Goose?

GOOSE: You know, same old, nothing much changes around here.

JAKE: Some things do.

GOOSE: Look, I've got to go meet a friend, so . . .

JAKE: I've talked to Shyanne . . . I heard what happened to Mike.

GOOSE: I gotta go.

JAKE: What's the rush? You're not embarrassed to be seen talking to me, are you?

GOOSE: Why should I? I'm not the one who has anything to be embarrassed about.

JAKE: What you did is disgusting.

GOOSE: What I did? If you are talking about last summer, it was you who was disgusting; lying to me, making me look like a fool, trying to steal my guy.

JAKE: I didn't steal Mike because he wasn't yours to begin with! You don't care about anybody but yourself.

GOOSE: I treated you like my little brother and—and—you're a fag and you didn't tell me!

JAKE: How was I supposed to tell you when everyone around here hates fags?

GOOSE: Well, that's your problem, not mine.

JAKE: Don't be ignorant, Goose, you know what I'm talking about!

GOOSE: Stop yelling. People are looking.

JAKE: I don't care; let them look. Yeah, take a good look at the fag. Why don't you take a picture, it lasts longer?

GOOSE: If you don't leave me alone I am going to slug you.

JAKE: Go ahead, I don't give a shit. You ruined Mike's life just because you couldn't have him and it doesn't even bother you. You're so fucking selfish. It's always about you, you, you! There was something special between me and Mike and you destroyed it. I hope someday I can forgive you but right now I'm just so ashamed that you're my cousin. I don't care what people think of me anymore. . . you can call me queer, fag, homo, whatever you like, but in my heart I'm proud of who I am and no one can take that away from me.

BETTY MOSES AND JAKE MEET

BETTY MOSES: Hello? Who are you? What do you want?

JAKE: Betty Moses? Are you Betty Moses? I'm Jake. Jake Pinashi.

BETTY MOSES: Do I know you?

JAKE: Sorry, no, but I was a friend of Mike's and your niece Shyanne told me where you live. I was away. I just got back and I heard about . . . I just came by to say that I am sorry for your loss and wanted to give you my condolences.

BETTY MOSES: Ohh . . . You're him, aren't you?

JAKE: I'm sorry?

BETTY MOSES: You're Jake? Yes . . . Michael wrote about you.

JAKE: He wrote about me?

BETTY MOSES: Yes . . . the letter he left . . . he wrote that you were special, like him. Are you?

Beat.

It's okay, I didn't understand before, but now I do. Mikey felt trapped. He had no one to love. No one to tell . . . his friends on the hockey team . . . they found out . . . he was different . . . he was their best player and they treated him like dirt. It was all he had and they didn't want him anymore. I didn't know and . . . then I found him . . . my son . . . he couldn't tell me when he was alive. I had a dream, you know, before it happened . . . a strange dream where a creature came to me . . . and whispered in my ear a word . . . a word I didn't understand: Agokwe. It means within the man there is a woman . . . not one spirit but two . . . two-spirited. It means you're special. Isn't that lovely? Isn't it? You know, sometimes we think we're so smart but we are stupid. We dirty everything, the land, the air, the water . . . and ourselves. We make those around us who are special feel dirty because we are stupid! In the old days we didn't waste people the way we do now . . . everybody was welcome, everybody had a place. Without Mikey our hockey team doesn't win anymore . . . Mikey's gone but you're still here, so you have to be strong for both of you . . . ice and fire . . . not one spirit but two.

NANABUSH: Can you see me? You can see me, right? Of course you can see me! But the only reason you can see me is because I choose for you to see me! I am Nanabush. I'm a trickster. I'm the trickster, the trickster of tricksters!

He bows to the audience.

Have you got it? You got it, right? And now I want you to act on it. And tell your friends, and tell your friends to tell their friends, and tell their friends to tell their friends. That way we can all live together like a nice big happy family!

The end.

NOTES ON THE CONTRIBUTORS

Sharon M. Day is an Ojibwe writer, musician, and artist who considers the community the ensemble and canvas for her work. She created the Ogitchidag Gikinooamagad Theater Program in 1990, which has run performances every year but one since its inception. She is an editor of *Sing, Whisper, Shout, Pray! Feminist Visions for a Just World*, a composer, a vocalist with the Neeconis Women Singers, a winner of juried art awards from Southwest Museum, and was featured in *Women in Love: Portraits of Lesbian Mothers and Their Families*. Ms. Day is also the executive director and a founding member of the Indigenous Peoples Task Force, which began in 1987. Under her leadership the organization has built a community-housing complex and established community gardens. Ms. Day was the lead walker for the Mother Earth Water Walk, carrying ocean water from the Gulf of Mexico to the shores of Lake Superior in 2011, and led the Mississippi River Water Walk in March 2013, carrying the clean, fresh water from the head waters of Lake Itasca to the dead zones of the Mississippi at Fort Jackson, Louisiana—a journey of 1,754 miles. The walks are to pray for the water and to listen to and tell the stories of people concerned about the waters. We are the water.

Tomson Highway was born in a snow bank on the Manitoba/Nunavut border to a family of nomadic caribou hunters. He had the great privilege of growing up in two languages, Cree, his mother tongue, and Dene, the language of the neighbouring "nation," a people with whom they roamed and hunted. Today, he enjoys an international career as a playwright, novelist, and pianist/songwriter. His best-known works are the plays *The Rez Sisters, Dry Lips Oughta Move To Kapuskasing, Rose,* and *Ernestine Shuswap Gets Her Trout* and the best-selling novel *Kiss of the Fur Queen.* For many years he ran Canada's premiere Native theatre company, Native Earth Performing Arts, out of which has emerged an entire generation of professional Native playwrights, actors, and, more indirectly, the many other Native theatre companies that now dot the country. He divides his year equally between a cottage in northern Ontario (near Sudbury, from whence comes his partner of twenty-five years) and a seaside apartment in the south of France, at both of which locales he is currently at work on his second novel.

Richard William Hill is a curator, critic, and associate professor of art history at York University. His research focuses primarily, but not exclusively, on historical and contemporary art created by Indigenous North American artists. As a curator at the Art Gallery of Ontario, he oversaw the museum's first substantial effort to include Indigenous North American art and ideas in permanent collection galleries. He also curated *Kazuo Nakamura: A Human Measure* at the AGO in 2004, co-curated with Jimmie Durham *The American West* at Compton Verney, UK, in 2005, and *The World Upside Down*, which originated at the Walter Phillips Gallery at the Banff Centre in 2006 and toured across Canada. Professor Hill's essays on art have appeared in numerous books, exhibition catalogues, and periodicals. He has a long association with the art magazine *FUSE*, where he was a member of the board and editorial committee for many years and now writes a regular column reviewing recent art exhibitions. He is currently revising a book on the problem of agency in the art of Jimmie Durham, the subject of his Ph.D. thesis.

Falen Johnson is Mohawk and Tuscarora from Six Nations. She is a writer, dramaturge, and actor. Her first play, *Salt Baby*, has been staged with Native Earth Performing Arts, Planet IndigenUS, and the Next Stage Festival. Selected theatre acting credits include *The Only Good Indian . . .* ; *Triple Truth; A Very Polite Genocide; Death of a Chief; Tombs of the Vanishing Indian; The Ecstasy of Rita Joe; The River; Tout Comme Elle;* and *Where the Blood Mixes.* Falen is a graduate of George Brown Theatre School. She is currently the executive director for the Indigenous Performing Arts Alliance (www.ipaa.ca).

Jean O'Hara recently earned her Ph.D. in Theatre and Performance Studies at York University. The primary focus of her work is devised ensemble-based theatre that addresses socio-political issues. She has been a collaborator with Klamath Theatre Project, Native Earth Performing Arts, Centre for Indigenous Theatre, and the Alianait Arts Festival. She also co-created a short film with Wiyot filmmaker Michelle Hernandez. Jean has a background in physical theatre and has worked with the San Francisco Mime Troupe and the Dell'Arte International School of Physical Theatre. She has also studied and utilized Augusto Boal's theatre for social justice both in the community and the classroom. Jean has been directing and teaching theatre for the past fifteen years and her research interests include Indigenous theatre and representation and queer performance.

Adrian Stimson is a member of the Siksika (Blackfoot) Nation in southern Alberta. He is an interdisciplinary artist with a BFA with distinction from the Alberta College of Art and Design and an M.F.A. from the University of Saskatchewan. Recent exhibits and performances include

Brave Seduction at Queer City Cinema, Regina; *Beyond Redemption* at the Mendel Art Gallery; *Photo Quai* at the Musée du quai Branly, Paris; and *Unmasking* at the Canadian Cultural Centre in Paris, France.